Violin Making
A Guide for the Amateur

By Bruce Ossman

Fox Chapel Publishing Co. Inc.
1970 Broad Street
East Petersburg, PA 17520

©*1999, 2000 (second printing) by Fox Chapel Publishing Co., Inc.*

Publisher:	Alan Giagnocavo
Project Editor:	Ayleen Stellhorn
Layout:	Chuck Golding

Illustrations and Patterns by the author

ISBN # 1-56523-091-4

To order a copy of this book, please send check or money order for cover price plus $3.00 shipping to:

Fox Chapel Book Orders
1970 Broad Street
East Petersburg, PA 17520

Try your bookseller first!

Printed in China

Table of Contents

Chapter 1
Background and Structure

Background on the Violin

The violin evolved in Renaissance Italy with many luthiers contributing to its development over a long period. By the time of such masters as Amati, Stradivari and Guarneri, the violin had assumed physical and acoustic characteristics that were nearly identical to those of the violins being made today. It is commonly believed that violins of that time have never been surpassed in beauty or performance.

Structure of the Violin

Like any musical instrument, the violin is a device used to produce and amplify pleasing sounds. Essentially, it is a lightweight but strong wooden box with an extended neck on which are mounted four tensioned strings. These strings are caused to vibrate primarily by drawing a wooden bow strung with horsehair across the strings and sometimes by plucking the strings with fingers.

Either by conscious design or the result of form following function, the violin somewhat resembles the human body. Many of the terms used to describe the parts of a violin reflect that fact. Some early instruments even featured carved representations of human faces at the end of the neck, and the *scroll,* also found there, may symbolize human hair. The *corpus* (body) has the shape of a torso with a narrow *center bout* or waist, an expanded *lower bout* (hips), and a narrower *upper bout* (shoulders). The *belly* (top plate) and the *back* (bottom plate) form very complex arching shapes. The belly is made from spruce or pine and is carved on both surfaces so that it is reduced to a thickness of just a few millimeters. Two elegant *f*-shaped *sound holes* are cut through each side of this plate in the waist area. The back plate varies in thickness from approximately 5 millimeters in the middle to about 2 millimeters at the edge. It is usually made from maple although other hardwoods are sometimes substituted. The curved *ribs* (sides) are 2-millimeter thick pieces of maple that have been bent to shape. The ribs are strengthened at the inside edges by pine *lining strips*. Small *blocks* of pine or spruce reinforce the front and back ends of the body and also the four corners. A narrow groove is cut close to the edges of the belly and the back plates in order to hold decorative and strengthening strips of wood known as *purfling*. The *neck*, fastened to the upper end of the body, is usually cut from a block of maple. Its far end opens into a *pegbox* that is terminated by the gracefully carved scroll.

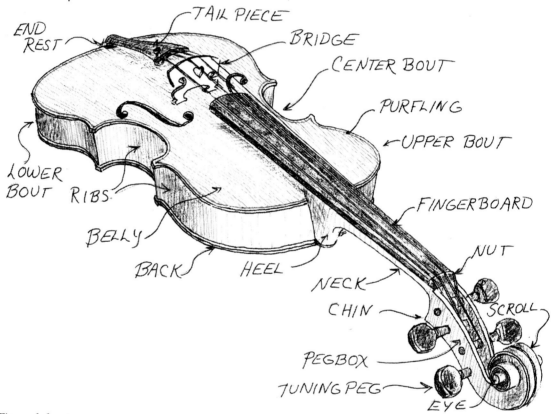

Figure 1-1

Ebony, either solid or veneered, is the traditional wood for the curved *fingerboard* which is glued to the top of the neck and extends toward a point near the forward ends of the *f*-holes. The small raised *nut* at the upper end of the fingerboard, the *end rest* at the back of the body, and the *tuning pegs* are also made of ebony or a similar hardwood. The four *strings*, once made of sheep gut, are now usually metal. They extend from the tuning pegs over the rounded nut that holds them slightly above the fingerboard, to the curved upper edge of the *bridge*, a thin piece of maple standing upright on the belly. Only the downward force of the strings holds the bridge in place. Each string is fastened at the other end to an ebony or plastic *tailpiece* that is tethered by heavy gut or nylon cord to an ebony *tail pin* at the lower end of the body.

When the strings are brought up to pitch (G, D, A, and E) by turning the pegs, a total longitudinal force of over 50 pounds is created. There is a downward force of about 20 pounds acting through the bridge to the belly plate below. This downward force would cause the belly to collapse were it not for the strengthening *bass bar*. This is a long, narrow strip of spruce or pine glued lengthwise to the underside of the belly below the bass string foot of the bridge. Under the treble-string foot a thin spruce rod known as the *soundpost* is loosely wedged in an upright position between the belly and back plates. The sound post serves as a compression strut and also as a fulcrum for plate vibration. With the exceptions of the soundpost, tuning pegs and the bridge, most of the violin parts are held together with glue. In some early violins, nails helped to secure the neck to the body.

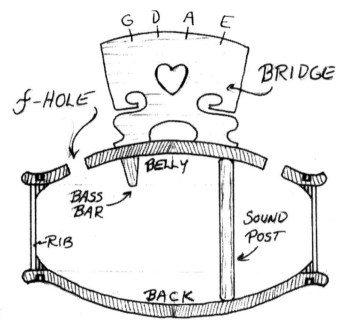

Figure 1-2

Acoustics of the Violin

The acoustics of a violin are very complex and seemingly mysterious, but as in any musical instrument, the laws of physics determine the sounds produced. A string is set into vibrating motion by drawing the horsehair of a bow across it at a short distance forward from where the string crosses the bridge. The string vibrates in a horizontal plane at a certain *resonant frequency* that is dependent on the string's length, tension and mass. In addition to the string's main resonant frequency, there will be a large number of partial waves (*overtones or harmonics*). All the sounds produced by the violin must originate from these string tones or overtones. However, since the string has a very small surface area, it is not able to transfer much sound energy directly to the air. The violin transfers the very weak, almost inaudible vibrations of the strings to much larger surfaces that will amplify the sound by setting more air into vibration.

The outside surfaces of the plates generate most of the sound. The *f*-holes serve to create an area of weakness in the belly so that its center section vibrates more easily. When the string vibrates in its horizontal plane, some of its energy is transferred to the bridge, which is forced into a rocking motion around its vertical center line. The bridge transfers some of the force through its two widely spaced feet to the belly. Since the feet of the bridge do not leave the top plate, the belly is forced into a complex, twisting motion. Some of this energy is carried to the back plate through the sound post and ribs. All the vibrating parts then generate sound waves that travel through the air.

The transfer of string vibration into the *forced vibration* of the violin parts is not the only factor in the production of sound. If that were the case, all the tones and harmonics generated by the string would be projected equally. However, just as each string at a certain length and tension will have its own resonant frequency, so will each component of the violin. Even the air inside the body will resonate at a certain frequency. When energy is transferred through the bridge to the violin body, most of the instrument is forced into *non-resonant* vibration. If a particular part of the violin happens to have a *natural resonance* that is the same as a tone produced by a string, that sound will receive greater amplification. If no part of the violin has a natural resonance that matches a particular string tone, then that tone will sound relatively weak. The perfect violin would be 100% efficient in transforming all of the energy provided by the player into sound and it would amplify every tone and harmonic equally. Such a flawless acoustic violin has never been created.

The "old masters" did not achieve perfection, although they came wonderfully close. Violins, even from the same maker, often show variations in plate thickness from instrument to instrument, probably as a result of a continuing attempt to balance tonal response. Modern acoustical engineers, when designing "high fidelity" stereo systems, combine electronic woofers, tweeters, and mid-range speakers to accomplish full-range reproduction of sound. In much the same way, most violins, ancient and new, show thickness variations within each plate in an attempt to produce resonance in as many frequencies as possible.

Although the method used to build a violin today is essentially the same as it was in the past, historians disagree about the sequencing of the steps involved. The Renaissance era masters, using only hand tools, achieved wonderful results. Perhaps because of their desire to protect trade secrets, they left few written records. In classic violins, the thin ribs and linings were probably bent to the desired curves after first being heated. The ribs were then temporarily fastened to a form, or mold, and strengthening linings were glued into place on their inside edges. As the top and bottom plates were carved to shape with gouges and scrapers, their thickness was measured with calipers. Rapping the plates with a knuckle gave certain "tap-tones" by which the masters determined when the carving was finished. Many modern makers still use these methods, but power tools now speed up the carving and, sometimes, the plates are "tuned" with the aid of electronic devices. In the earliest violins the base of the neck was shaped to fit the outside surface of the front ribs. In addition to glue, Stradivari also used three nails driven from inside the front block into the base of the neck to help secure the neck to the body. In modern violins, the neck-to-body joint is made stronger by "dovetailing" the heel of the neck into a tapered opening cut into the upper ribs and block. Most likely, no one uses nails any more, but one or more small screws in addition to a modern "super glue," can make the neck-to-body joint very rigid.

Dense, fine-grained "tone woods" have always been highly prized for the brilliant sounds they produce. Maple and spruce have been the traditional woods, but today, some makers are experimenting with substitutes, such as cherry, birch and mahogany.

There is much speculation about secret varnishes that supposedly gave the old violins their distinctive sound. In reality, a violin is often at its best without any varnish at all. Varnish does protect the surface from the elements, but the real challenge is to find a finish that is the least damaging to the sound quality. Some makers today are using only oil-based finishes that allow freer movement of the violin surfaces.

The slight changes evident in modern violins were brought about mostly by the standardization of musical notes at higher frequencies than were the fashion in Baroque times and by the increase in average human stature. Violin necks became longer and were attached at an increased angle to the body. Higher string tensions necessitated the stronger dovetail joint between the neck and the body. Because of the changed neck angle, a higher bridge was needed and that caused an increased downward pressure on the top plate. A heavier bass bar had to be added to prevent the collapse of the instrument.

As a result of these changed requirements, it is very rare to find an ancient instrument that is still in its original condition. Most old violins have been taken apart and refitted with new bass bars, necks and fingerboards. In some cases, restorers have even had the audacity to change the thickness of the plates. In addition to these modifications, the wood itself will have undergone chemical and physical changes. The passage of centuries will have exposed instruments to deterioration caused by oxidation, humidity, temperature extremes, insect attack and accident. Constant string tension for hundreds of years will have caused many violin plates and ribs to deform or even crack.

Because sophisticated measuring devices did not exist until recent times, it can't be determined if the performance of a classic violin is better or worse today than when it was first created. It is likely that its sound has changed. Some violins made today are just as good if not better than those made by the old masters but these too will change over time. We now have the means to detect and measure any changes that do occur.

Chapter 2
Preparation of Materials

Violin makers today tend to be very conservative and many feel that an instrument must be made with exactly the same materials and methods established centuries ago. These makers go to great lengths and expense to obtain the finest maple, spruce and ebony. The gouges, hand saws, finger planes and building forms must be the same as those used by the old masters. Even the presumed sequencing of steps in the building process is duplicated as closely as possible. They do much research into trying to uncover the long lost secrets of wood treatment and "tone-enhancing" varnishes.

All of these things are of great interest to historians or professional luthiers but for someone attempting a first violin without benefit of apprenticeship under a master, these details can be intimidating. Building a violin entirely in the traditional manner may indeed yield superior results, but a good first instrument can be made with modern tools, less expensive materials, and a few changes in technique that simplify some of the procedures.

The directions in this chapter and the next will enable you to make a violin in a logical sequence, beginning with the preparation of materials and continuing with step-by-step procedures in shaping and assembling the parts.

You may choose to make a violin entirely with hand tools, but if you have access to a band saw and a drill press, the work will be much faster.

Making the curved violin ribs and linings has always been one of the most difficult stages of building. In this plan, the ribs and linings will be easily laminated from strips of 1/32" maple, birch, or mahogany veneer. However, if you are experienced in the heat-bending of wood and you prefer the traditional method of rib making, quarter-cut maple can be planed down to a thickness of $1/16''$ and then bent to shape over a heated metal bar. Whichever method you use, the finished ribs will be glued to the corner and end blocks that are held in place on a slightly modified Stradivari-type building form. The only significant changes in the form are in the area where the corner blocks are temporarily attached. They will be set deeper into the form (mold) so that gluing the linings to the ribs will be much easier. Small "C" clamps are usually used to hold the blocks and ribs to the mold during gluing but these expensive items can be eliminated by using wooden dowels and elastic bands.

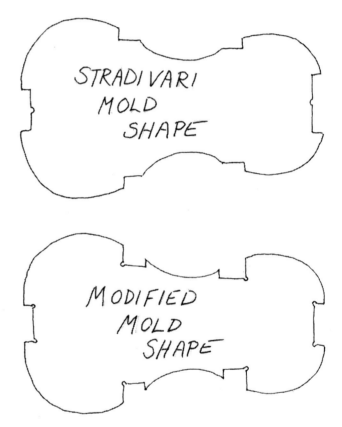

Figure 2-1

It is not advisable to buy costly "tone woods" for a first violin. If you search through stacks of spruce and maple boards at your local lumber yard, you will eventually find some well-seasoned quarter-sawn planks that can be used for the top and bottom plates. Ebony is expensive and possibly toxic to work with; instead, hard maple can be used for making the fingerboard and some other fittings.

To shape the plates you will need scrapers and gouges (#5 sweep in $3/4''$ and $1/4''$ sizes would be good choices). A carving knife with interchangeable small blades and gouges will be needed to carve the *f*-holes and the scroll.

Luthier's clamps are simple to make from carriage bolts, wing nuts, and dowel rods. If available, spring clamps are preferable because they are much faster and easier to use.

Hundreds of modern glues exist and many of them are stronger than the wooden parts they join. However, old style hide glues are still recommended for joining the plates to the ribs and the fingerboard to the neck as sometimes a violin must be taken apart for repairs.

In most violins the bass bar is a separate piece of wood that is carefully shaped to fit the inside surface of the belly plate before it is glued in place. In the building process described here, a choice can be made to shape the bass bar during the plate hollowing process so that it becomes an integral part of the belly. This is easier to do and it will never vibrate loose.

Many modern luthiers recommend that the neck be fitted into the body after both the top and bottom plates are glued in place. This is extremely hard to do because of the dovetail joint. Stradivari's violin necks are secured from inside with nails which shows that he did not favor that practice. In this plan, the belly plate is first glued to the ribs, then the neck is fitted and glued. A single reinforcing screw replaces the Stradivarian nails. After the heel of the neck is cut to the correct length, the bottom plate is glued on to close the body.

Measurements in this text alternate between the metric and the English systems. By tradition, the dimensions of individual violin parts have long been given in metric units. Unfortunately, the U.S. continues to produce tools and materials based on the old English standards. Thus, the carving turntable requires ¾" plywood, a hole drilled in the front block is made with a ⅛" drill bit, veneer sheeting is usually ¹/₃₂" thick, the back plate varies in thickness from 2.9 mm to 4.4 mm and the end rest is 4.0 cm long.

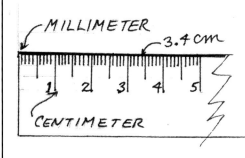

Even though the basic design of the violin has been fixed for centuries, there is still room for experiment and possible improvements. For example, some avant-guarde violins being made today have wildly asymmetrical shapes. Electronic violins are in a separate class entirely.

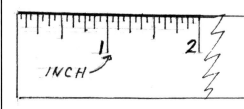

You will probably make more than one violin and you may eventually decide to examine such questions as:

1. What happens to a violin's performance if the bass bar shape is modified?

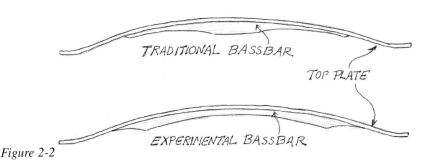

Figure 2-2

2. Would an internal brace between the top and bottom blocks add longitudinal strength and allow the plates to vibrate more freely?

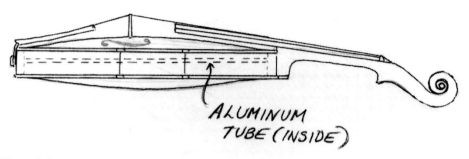

Figure 2-3

3. Could the design of the bridge be simplified and improved? Decreasing the mass at the top of the bridge might permit a faster response to string vibration.

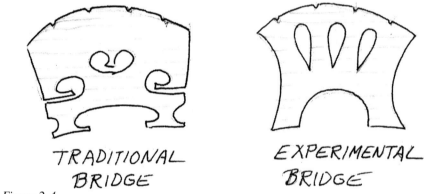

Figure 2-4

There are many other subtle changes you will want to make on a second or third violin. Perhaps you will be the first to create the perfect acoustic instrument, one that reproduces all frequencies equally well. First, it will be informative to build a violin in a more traditional way.

The Body Form

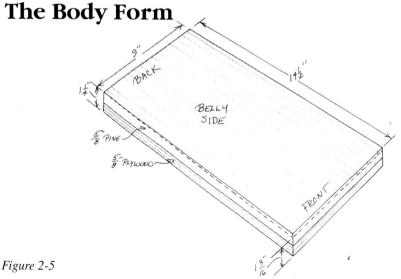

Figure 2-5

1. The ribs (sides) of the finished violin will taper slightly from back to front. Obtain two ⅝" thick boards with the dimensions shown in Figure 2-5. The bottom board should be warp resistant plywood. The top board must be wood such as pine that can be planed so that the front edge of the combined boards is 1³⁄₁₆" thick.

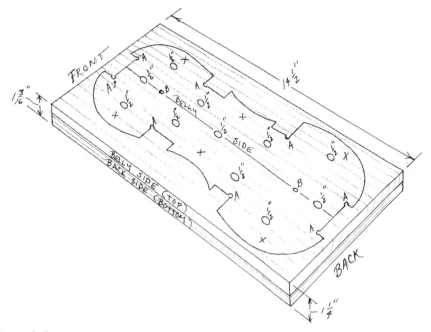

Figure 2-6

2. Transfer the full-sized pattern for the body form to the surface of the top board (Figure 2-6). Do this by gluing the pattern to the wood or tracing through carbon paper.

3. Use "C" clamps to temporarily hold the boards together. Drill guide holes for six 1" flat-head screws at the points marked "X" on the pattern. Countersink the heads so that they will not project above the surface of the form. Turn in the screws to lock the boards together. Remove the "C" clamps.

4. Drill the eleven ½" holes through both boards.

5. Drill ¼" holes at the eight corners marked "A".

6. With the boards still fastened together, use a band saw with a ⅛" blade to cut around the outer shape of the form.

7. Remove the 6 screws and separate the 2 halves of the form. Drill and tap two holes for ⅜"x20"x1" machine screws at points "B" in the top plate only!

8. Reinsert the 6 flat-head screws and lock the two halves of the form together.

9. Mark the top half of the form "belly" and the bottom half "back."

Corner and End Blocks

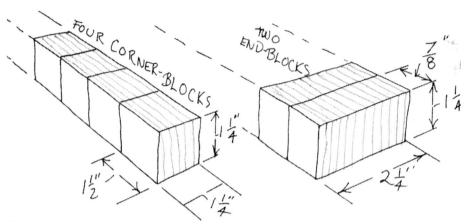

Figure 2-7

From close-grained pine or spruce cut 4 corner and 2 end blocks to the dimensions shown in Figure 2-7.

Rib Forms

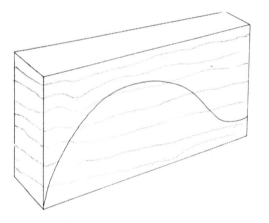

Figure 2-8

Cut the lower bout, center bout, and upper bout rib forms from 1⅜" thick slabs of wood (any type) to the shapes shown on the patterns. Do the cutting on the curved solid lines with a band saw.

Veneer Rib-Strips

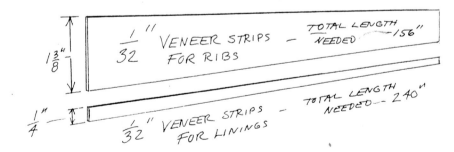

Figure 2-9

Cut 1⅜" wide strips from straight-grained ¹⁄₃₂" thick mahogany or maple veneer. The cutting can be easily done with a band saw. Lacking that, place the veneer sheet flat on a glass surface and cut downward with a thin, sharp blade. A total length of about 156 inches is needed.

Veneer Lining Strips

Cut ¼" wide strips from the ¹⁄₃₂" veneer sheet. A total length of about 240 inches is needed (Figure 2-9).

Dowels Used in Body Form

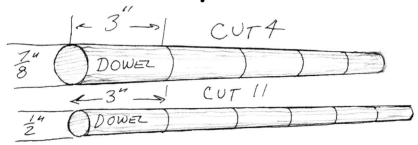

Figure 2-10

Cut four 3" lengths of ⅞" dowel and eleven 3" lengths of ½" dowel.

Top (Belly) Plate

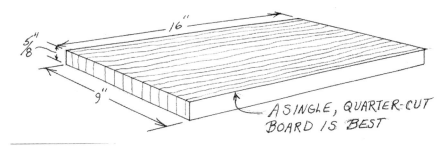

Figure 2-11

Choose a 9" wide, close-grained, quarter-cut, knot-free pine, spruce, or Douglas fir board. Have it planed down to a thickness of ⅝".

Figure 2-12

If a 9" wide board cannot be located, two smaller width, quarter-cut boards must be glued together.

Bottom (Back) Plate

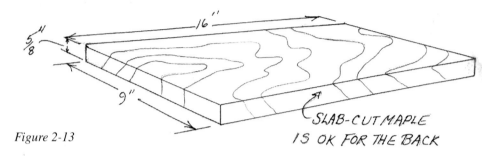

Figure 2-13

The best wood for the back is quarter-cut maple, as in Figures 2-11 or 2-12. Slab-cut maple may be used for the back, but it must be a single board for best appearance.

End Rest

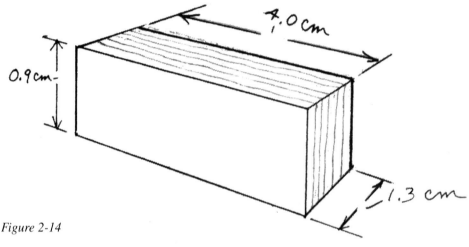

Figure 2-14

Cut the end-rest block from ebony or hard maple (Figure 2-14).

Neck/Pegbox/Scroll Block

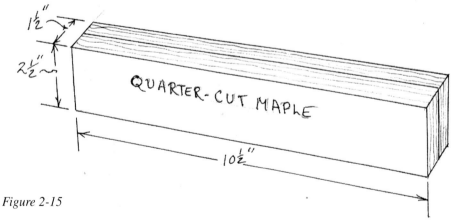

Figure 2-15

Cut a piece of straight-grained maple (quarter-cut wood is best) to the dimensions shown in Figure 2-15. Two pieces of ³/₄" wood may be glued together to give the required 1¹/₂" thickness. This has the double advantage of adding strength and providing a needed centerline.

Fingerboard Blank

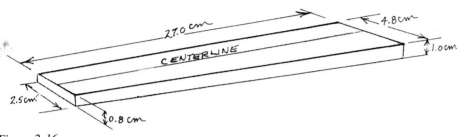

Figure 2-16

Purchase a partially-shaped ebony fingerboard or cut hard maple to the dimensions shown in Figure 2-16.

Nut

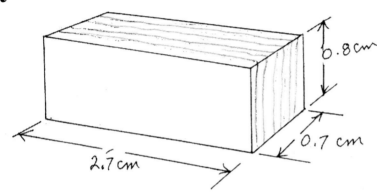

Figure 2-17

Cut a piece of ebony or hard maple to the dimensions shown in Figure 2-17.

Carving Turntable

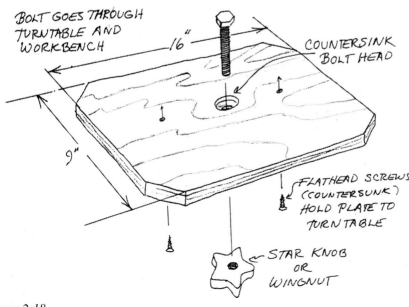

Figure 2-18

Fashion the device shown in Figure 2-18 to hold the top and bottom plates during the carving process. The bolt can be of any diameter but must be long enough to pass through a hole drilled in the top of your workbench. A star knob at the other end is most convenient but a large nut or wing nut will work. The two flat-head screws which penetrate from the bottom must hold the plate securely but must not be so long that they pierce the top of the plate.

Luthier's Clamps

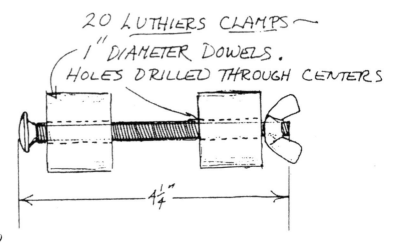

Figure 2-19

You will need about twenty of these easy-to-make clamps which will be used to hold the plates to the ribs while glue dries out. Cut an old broom handle into 1 inch lengths and drill a hole through each (Figure 19). Spring clamps like the one shown at left are much easier to use. You will need to purchase about 14 clamps.

Sound Post Inserter and Setter

Figure 2-20

1. Make an inserter from a piece of heavy wire with 2 small pins tied or soldered in place as shown.

2. Cut a setter from a piece of galvanized tin. Use the pattern from the full-size plans section.

3. Both the inserter and the setter are bendable as needed so that the sound post can be positioned inside the finished violin through the right hand *f*-hole.

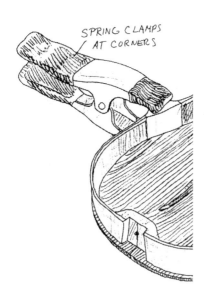

SPRING CLAMPS AT CORNERS

The tuning pegs, tailpiece, tailpin, bridge and purfling strips are usually purchased in a finished or semi-finished condition.

Chapter 3
Construction of the Violin

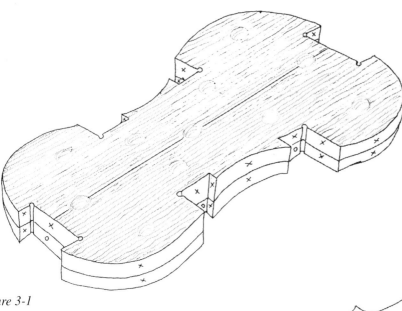

Figure 3-1

1. The corner and end blocks will be fastened temporarily by tack-gluing them to the lower section of the form and will be separated from the form after the ribs (sides) have been glued to the blocks. For this reason, the blocks should not fit tightly into the form recesses. Apply small droplets of glue to the lower part of the body form at the areas indicated "O". The areas marked "X" should not receive glue.

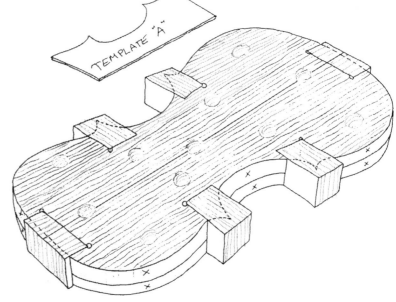

Figure 3-2

2. Place the form on a flat surface.

Slide the four corner and two end blocks into place and clamp with dowels and elastic bands or "C" clamps until the glue is dry

3. Use a file to bring the corner and end blocks level with the top and bottom of the form.

4. Use template "A" to trace the shapes of the corner points onto the four corner blocks.

5. Draw the curves on the end blocks so that they continue the curves of the form (Figure 3-2).

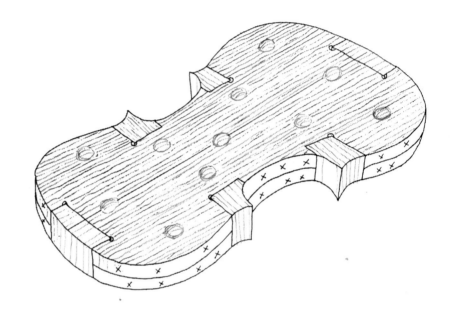

Figure 3-3

6. Use a band saw to trim the corner and end blocks to shape (Figure 3-3).

7. Line the contacting surfaces of the lower bout form with strips of waxed paper. Secure them with small pieces of tape.

8. The $1/32$" thick veneer should have been cut into $1\frac{3}{8}$" wide strips. Cut two pieces of veneer to a length of 28 cm.

9. Spread woodworking glue over one surface of one piece of veneer. Place the other strip of veneer over the glue-coated surface. Wipe away any excess glue that is squeezed out. Align the edges and then staple *one* end of the combined strips.

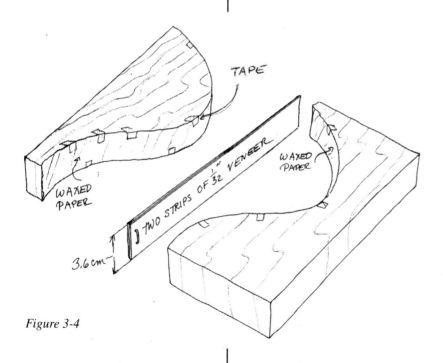

Figure 3-4

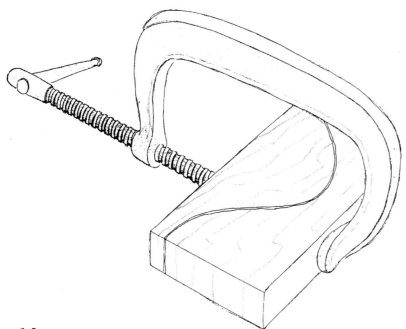

Figure 3-5

10. Place the combined strips between the mating edges of the form. Press the two parts of the form together and then clamp them tightly while the glue dries (Figure 3-5).

11. Repeat the process described in steps 7-10 for the other two bouts (the lengths of the veneer strips are indicated on the full-sized patterns for the forms).

12. When the 3 composite ribs are dry, remove them and use the same forms to make 3 more ribs.

13. Using a wax crayon or candle, rub over the edges of the body form where glue should *not* adhere (the areas in Figures 3-1, 3-2, and 3-3 marked "X"). The ribs will be glued only to the corner and end blocks.

14. Clamp the body form into a vise with one of the center bouts facing upward. Place one of the center ribs into the center bout of the form. Mark the areas of the rib that will contact the corner blocks (Figure 3-6).

15. Apply a thin layer of glue to the inside curves of the corner blocks. Also apply glue to the mating surfaces of the inner bout ribs.

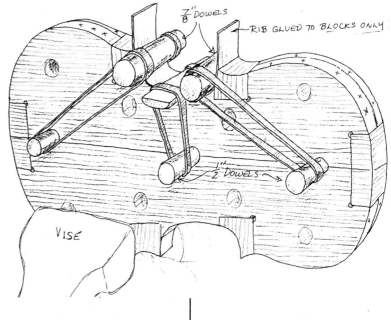

Figure 3-6

16. Press the center rib into place. Use a thin strip of veneer to scrape away any expressed glue. It is important that the ribs are not glued to the body form.

17. Use dowels, flat strips of wood, and numerous elastic bands to pull the center rib tightly against the corner blocks. Figure 3-6 shows only one band at each pressure point but five or six will be required to give sufficient force.

18. Glue the other center rib in place in the same manner. When the glue has dried, remove the elastic bands, dowels, and flat strips.

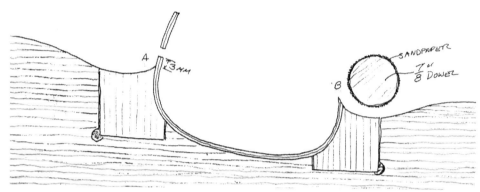

Figure 3-7

19. Use a band saw to trim the ends of the middle bouts about 3 mm beyond the points of the corner blocks (Figure 3-7A).

20. Use sandpaper wrapped around a ⅞" dowel to sand the edges of the center bout ribs so that the curves of the corner blocks continue outward (Figure 3-7B).

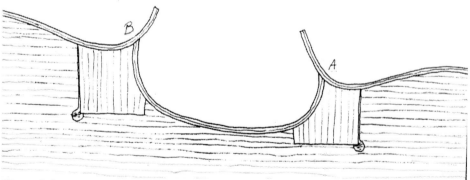

Figure 3-8

21. Glue the two upper bout ribs in place in the same manner. The joint where they meet at the front block does not need to be perfect because that area will be cut away later when the neck is installed. The upper ribs will temporarily extend beyond the center ribs as shown in Figure 3-8A.

22. Place the back ribs against the form and measure the exact length at the back join. Use the band saw to cut the ribs to that length.

23. Glue the lower bout ribs in place. These ribs overlap the center ribs as shown in Figure 3-8B.

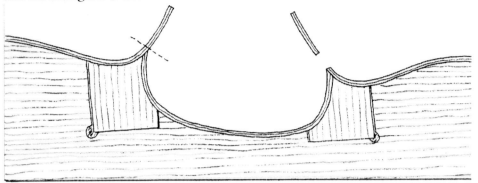

Figure 3-9

24. Use the band saw to trim the four corners as shown in Figure 3-9.

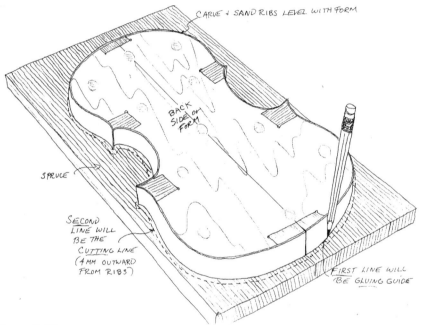

Figure 3-10

25. Carve and sand the ribs down to the level of the form on both sides (Figure 3-10). Use a very sharp knife and shave away the waste wood carefully. Watch the grain direction closely to avoid splitting the ribs.

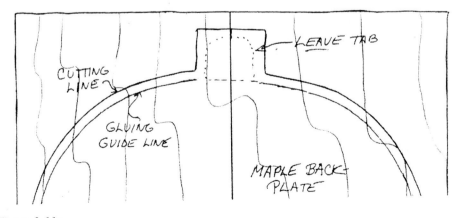

Figure 3-11

26. Place the side of the form and rib structure marked "belly" on top of the *spruce* board which will form the belly (top) of the instrument. Align the center join of the top board with the centerline of the form. Use a pencil to trace the outline of the form/rib assembly onto the board. This line is *not* a cutting line but it will serve later as a guide when the top is glued to the ribs.

27. Using a spacer, draw a second line around the form/rib structure. Make the second line 4 mm outward from the first line. This outer line will be the cutting line.

28. Place the side of the form/rib assembly marked "back" against the *maple* board. Repeat steps 26 and 27. Be sure to leave a tab (button) for the portion of the back which will eventually cover the base of the neck (Figure 3-11). The button is not merely ornamental but is essential in strengthening the neck-body join so that the large forces of a tensioned violin will not cause the neck to separate from the body.

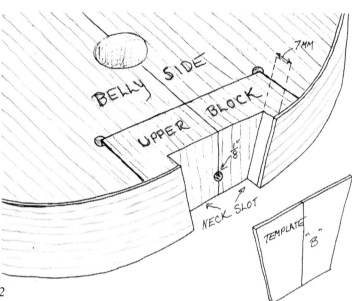

Figure 3-12

29. Use *Template B* to mark the ends of the front ribs for the tapered neck slot to be cut (Figure 3-12).

30. On both top and bottom, measure in 7 mm from the front of the form/rib assembly and draw lines at 90° to mark the depth of the neck slot in the block.

31. Fasten the form/rib assembly upright in a vise. Use a coping saw and a file to cut and shape the neck slot.

32. Drill a ⅛" diameter hole in the lower part of the front block (Figure 3-12). In Step #131, a screw will be inserted from inside the body to help hold the neck securely to the front block.

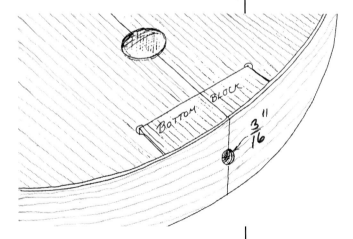

Figure 3-13

33. Reposition the form/rib assembly in the vise and drill a ³⁄₁₆" hole at the center point of the join of the back ribs and through the bottom block as shown in Figure 3-13. In Step #163 this hole will be enlarged with a ream so that the tail pin can be inserted.

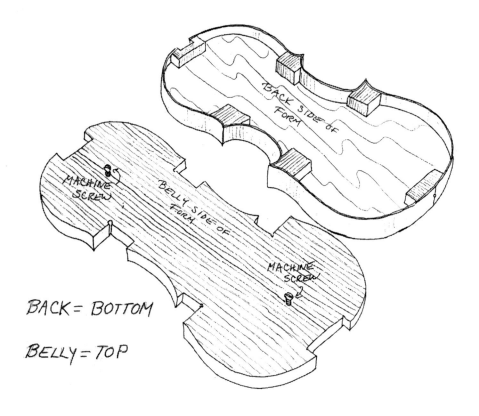

Figure 3-14

34. Remove the 6 flat-head screws that hold the two sections of the form together.

35. Insert the 2 machine screws in the matching holes in the top section of the form. Slowly turn them to lift the top part of the form free (Figure 3-14).

36. The bottom part of the form is left in place for the next few steps. However, be sure that the form can be easily released from the rib/block assembly at a later time! If the blocks were lightly glued to the form at the indicated places, a thin blade should separate them easily. If not, use a coping saw to separate the blocks from the form. The small holes drilled in the form at the corners of the blocks permit the insertion of the coping saw blade. Hold the form/rib assembly in a vise and saw the bases of the blocks where they contact the form. Do not damage the form as it can be used again in making more violins.

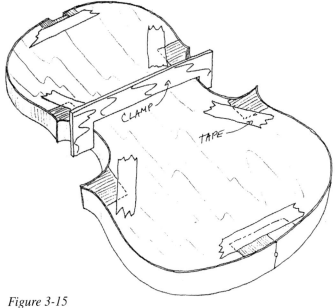

Figure 3-15

37. When the tack-glued blocks have been separated from the bottom half of the form, the rib/block assembly may spring away from the form. Turn the assembly over and use strips of tape and a plywood clamp to bring the ribs and blocks back into contact with the form (Figure 3-15).

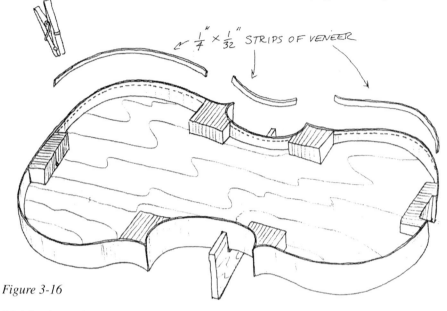

Figure 3-16

38. The bout linings will consist of three layers of ¼" wide, ¹⁄₃₂" thick veneer. Position the form/rib assembly as shown in Figure 3-16. Bend a strip of the veneer around the inside edge of one rib between the lower end-block and a lower corner block. Mark and cut the strip to that length. Glue the strip in place using numerous closely-spaced clothespins as clamps.

39. Repeat this process for the other lower bout lining.

40. Cut, glue, and clamp the center bout linings next.

41. Cut, glue, and clamp the linings for the upper bouts.

42. When the glue holding the first layer of linings is dry, repeat Steps 38-41 to add a second layer of veneer strips.

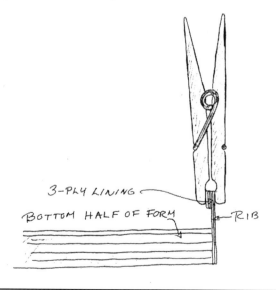

Figure 3-17

43. Cut, glue, and clamp a third layer of veneer strips on top of the second layer. These three layers form very strong, laminated linings on the upper edges of the ribs (Figure 3-17).

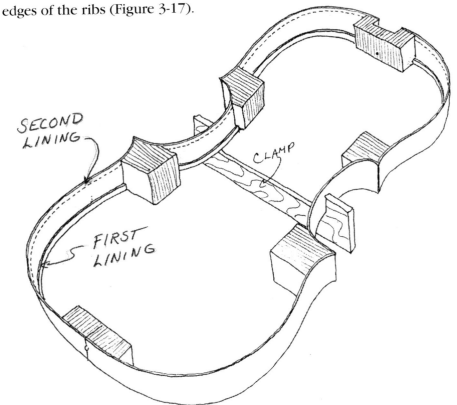

Figure 3-18

44. Remove the bottom half of the form from the block/rib assembly and replace the plywood clamp between the center bout ribs to ensure that the ribs maintain the correct spacing (Figure 3-18).

45. Repeat Steps 38-41 to install the three-ply, laminated rib liners on the other edge of the ribs.

46. Use a sharp blade and sandpaper on a sanding block to trim the linings to the level of the ribs (Figure 3-19).

47. Mark the corner and end blocks as shown by the dashed lines in Figure 3-19.

48. Hold the block/rib assembly in a vise and use a coping saw to cut away the waste wood of the corner and end blocks. Use a rounded file to smooth the inside surfaces.

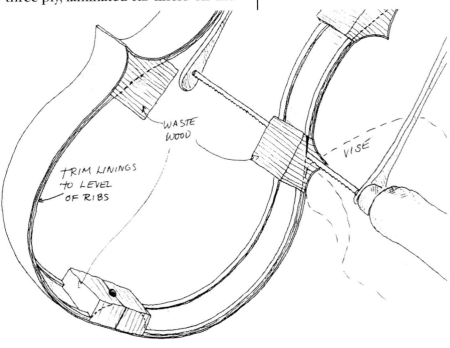

Figure 3-19

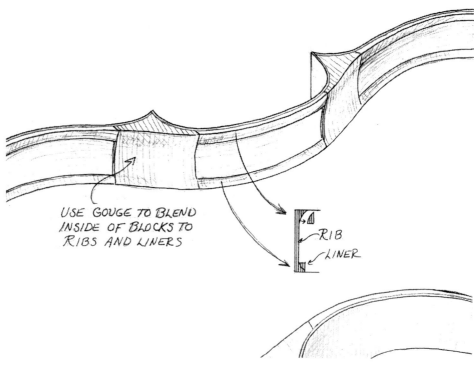

USE GOUGE TO BLEND
INSIDE OF BLOCKS TO
RIBS AND LINERS

RIB
LINER

Figure 3-20

49. Use a small gouge to shape the linings as shown in Figure 3-20.

50. Use a gouge to remove excess wood from the inside of the corner blocks.

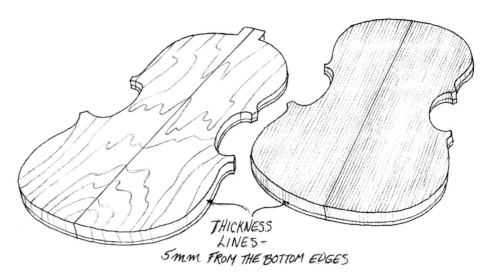

THICKNESS
LINES -
5mm FROM THE BOTTOM EDGES

Figure 3-21

51. The top (belly) and bottom (back) plates have already been marked in steps 26-28. The inner lines represent the actual shape of the ribs where they contact the plates. The outer lines, 4 mm beyond the inner lines, are the cutting lines. Use a ⅛" blade on the band saw so that the tight curves can be easily managed. Again, be sure to leave a tab on the back plate for later shaping of the button (Figure 3-21).

52. From the bottom edges of both plates mark a thickness of 5 mm at numerous points around the edges. Then, use a pencil to draw continuous lines around the plates to connect the points.

53. Before using gouges to shape the plates, remove much of the excess wood by sawing. First, use a pencil to mark the center lines of both plates.

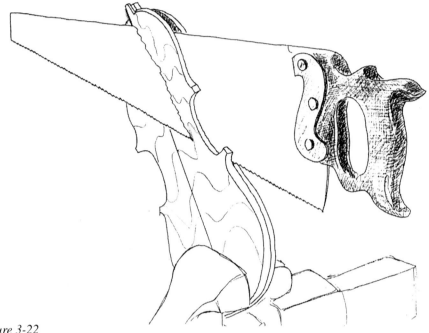

Figure 3-22

54. Clamp the maple back plate upright in a vise and make an angled saw-cut on the top side of the plate as shown in Figure 3-22. Do not cut below the edge thickness line or beyond the centerline on the plate. Make these cuts on both the left and the right sides of the plate top.

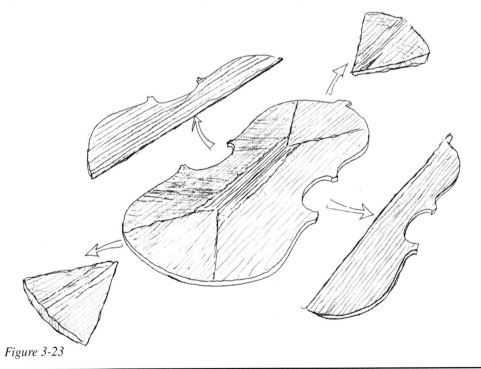

Figure 3-23

55. Use the saw to remove excess wood from the front and back ends of the plate top. The plate after rough shaping will resemble Figure 3-23.

56. Repeat the preliminary shaping process on the spruce belly plate.

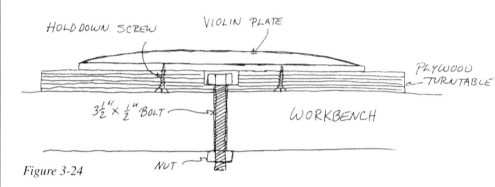

Figure 3-24

57. Using the two hold-down screws, fasten the back plate to the turntable as shown in Figure 3-24.

58. Use a very sharp ⅝", number 5 gouge to continue shaping of the plate. The first goal is to develop a generally rounded shape. Always use both hands on the gouge to maintain control as you carve. For the initial carving, push the gouge *away* from your body. Pulling the blade toward you, as in Figure 3-25, may be done only during the final trimming. If the gouge is properly sharpened, the carving will be easy and pleasurable, almost like carving hard wax. A dull blade will make the work dangerous and frustratingly difficult.

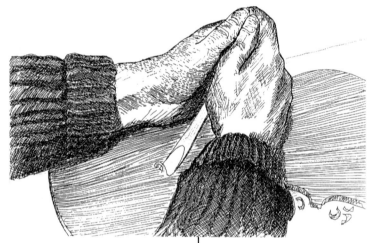

Figure 3-25

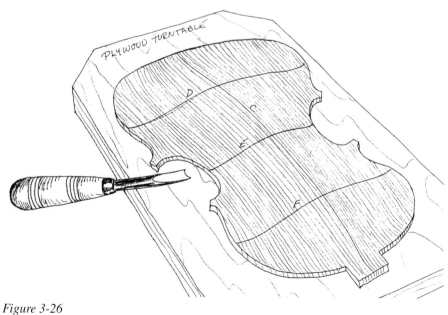

Figure 3-26

59. Continue carving with gouges until the plate takes on the shape indicated in Figure 3-26. The curves blend in a subtle, complex way. Use Templates C, D, E and F to aid in this process. The edges of the plates will be about 3.5 mm thick (see the dashed lines on pages 58 and 59). Do not go on until these shapes are as perfect as you can make them with gouges alone.

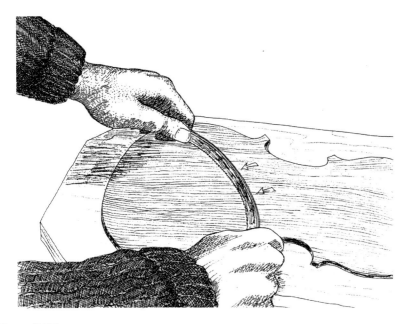

Figure 3-27

60. After the plate has been accurately shaped, scrape the surface in order to remove all traces of the gouge marks. A very effective tool is the flexible blade of a small knife-saw. If that is not available, several coarse-toothed, hacksaw blades held together side-by-side, with their teeth facing in opposite directions, will also work. Bend the blades, as needed, to fit the curvatures of the plate while drawing them toward you in diagonal sweeps (Figure 3-27).

61. When the gouge marks have nearly disappeared, switch to hacksaw blades with fine teeth. Then finish with the untoothed side of the blades to remove most of the scratch marks. Commercially made scrapers of varied shapes can be purchased in woodworking stores.

62. Use the same procedures to shape the spruce top plate.

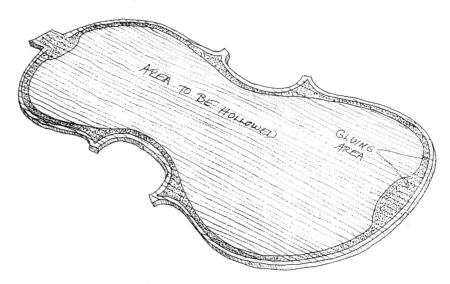

Figure 3-28

63. Place the side of the block/rib assembly marked "Back" against the flat side of the back plate. Trace the outlines of the ribs and blocks onto the plate. When the plate is hollowed, this area will remain untouched so as to present a flat, gluing surface, as shown by the stippled area in Figure 3-28.

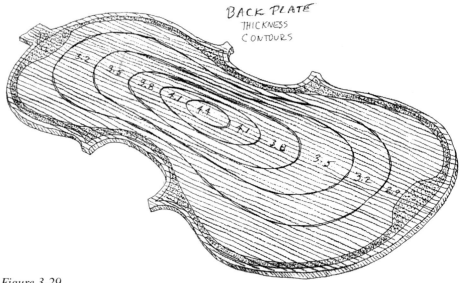

Figure 3-29

64. Use the full-sized back plate contour pattern and carbon paper to transfer the hollowing guidelines onto the flat surface of the back plate. Indicate the thickness for each zone (Figure 3-29).

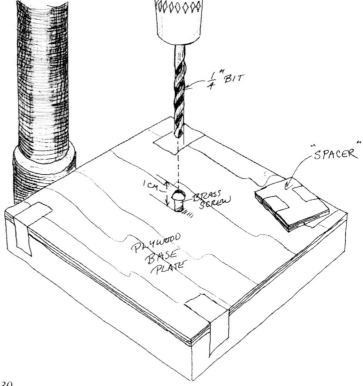

Figure 3-30

65. Tape a plywood base plate to the drill press table. Turn in a round-head, brass screw so that it lines up exactly with a ¼" drill bit (Figure 3-30).

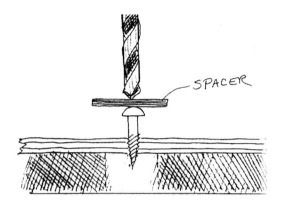

Figure 3-31

66. Set the drilling depth for a particular zone by using a stacked-paper spacer of the proper thickness (Figure 31).

67. Drill numerous, closely-spaced holes to the prescribed depth in each zone. Be sure to readjust the drilling depth when moving to a new zone (Figures 3-29 to 3-31).

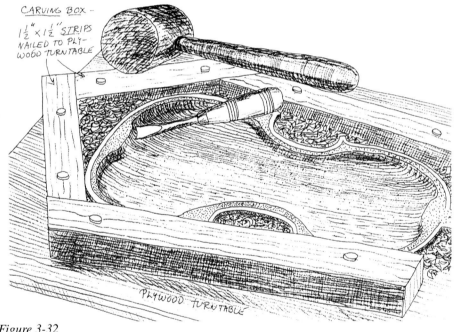

Figure 3-32

68. Place the drilled back plate in a carving box as shown in Figure 3-32. Use a bed of wood shavings in order to protect the finished outer surface of the plate. The carving box can be made to rotate like the turntable in Figure 3-24.

69. Begin to carve the waste wood from the underside of the plate. Drive the gouge with a mallet to ease the initial rough hollowing. Make the cuts at a slight angle to the grain direction to reduce the chance of the gouge sinking too deeply into the plate. Continue this carving until only small "dimples" remain from the drilled holes.

70. Use scrapers to smooth the inside surface of the plate until the dimples just disappear. The plate will now have the thickness shown in Figure 3-29.

If the plates were made from boards that were glued together (as in Fig. 2-12), you may wish to strengthen the joints after the plates are hollowed by gluing .5 in. squares of veneer on the inside surfaces of the joints. Space these studs about 2 in. apart and be sure that their grain direction is at right angles to the grain of the plate.

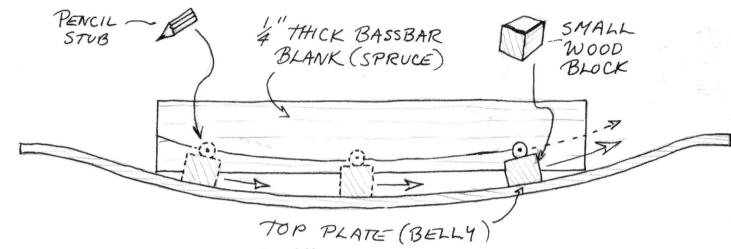

PENCIL STUB

¼" THICK BASSBAR BLANK (SPRUCE)

SMALL WOOD BLOCK

TOP PLATE (BELLY)

Figure 3-33

71. Steps 63-70 are repeated in hollowing the underside of the spruce top plate. If the bass bar is to be added as a separate piece, hollow the entire underside. If the bass bar is to be an integral part of the belly, be sure to indicate this when the pattern for the belly contours is transferred to the wood.

72. After the underside of the belly has been hollowed, use a chisel and a gouge to shape the bass bar strip until it conforms to template "G". If the bass bar is carved from a separate piece of wood, use fine-grained wood of the same type as the belly. Curve it for an *exact* fit with the underside of the plate (Figure 3-33) and clamp it in place as the glue dries.

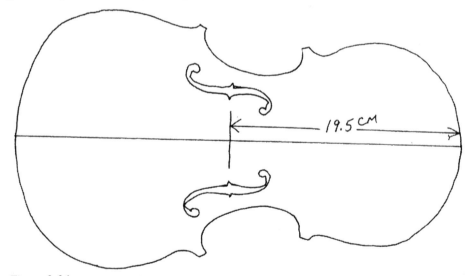

19.5 CM

Figure 3-34

73. Measure down 19.5 cm from the top of the spruce belly plate. Draw a light pencil line at right angles to the centerline of the plate. This pencil line will mark the future location of the bridge and will guide you in locating the *f*-holes (Figure 3-34).

74. Use *Template H* and a pencil to draw the shapes of the *f*-holes on both sides of the centerline.

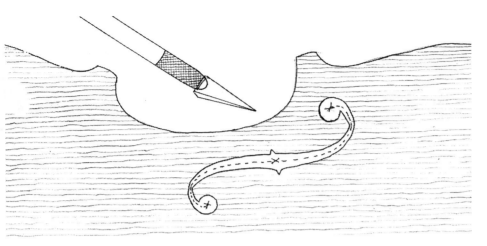

Figure 3-35

75. Drill ³/₁₆" holes at the points indicated by "X" on Figure 3-35. Be sure to use a backing of scrap wood so as not to split the plate when drilling.

76. Insert a fine-toothed coping saw blade or a modeling saw blade through one of the ³/₁₆" holes. Rest the plate at the edge of the workbench and with the blade hand-held, cut down the centerline of the *f*-hole as shown by the dashed line in Figure 3-35. Do *not* try to cut the *f*-hole to its final shape with the saw blade.

77. Use a small, sharp knife blade, to *carve* the *f*-holes to their finished shape. Take thin shavings and pay attention to the wood grain so as not to split the top.

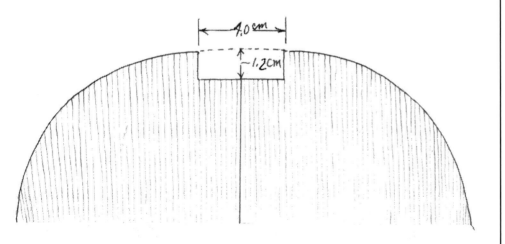

Figure 3-36

78. At the back edge of the spruce belly plate, mark the dimensions for the end rest cut-out as shown in Figure 3-36. Use the band saw to cut away this part of the plate.

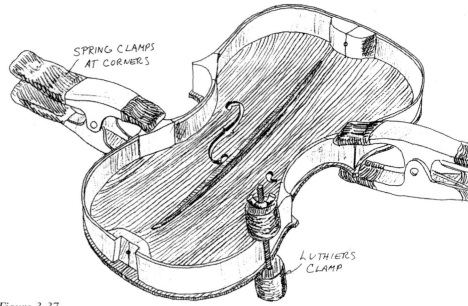

Figure 3-37

79. Apply a thin coat of glue to the edges of the ribs and blocks which have been marked "belly side."

80. Place the belly plate in contact with the glue-coated edge of the ribs. Check to see that the plate edge is equidistant from the ribs at all points. Use four spring clamps to hold the plate at the four corners (Figure 3-37).

81. Use additional spring clamps or luthier's clamps all around the edges to hold the belly plate against the ribs. Some glue will be squeezed out. Use a small strip of veneer to scrape away the excess glue. Then wipe away any remaining surface glue with a dampened cloth.

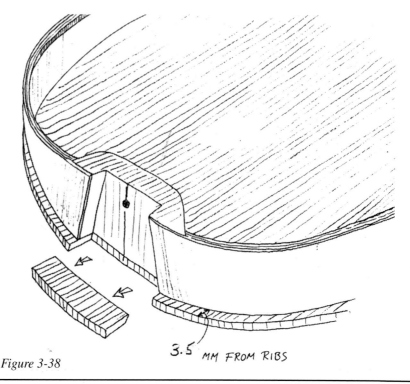

Figure 3-38

82. When the glue has dried, use a coping saw to cut away the small section of the belly plate that covers the top of the neck slot. Trim the edges with a flat file (Figure 3-38).

83. With a carving knife, file, and sanding block, trim the edges of the belly plate so that they project evenly 3.5 mm beyond the ribs.

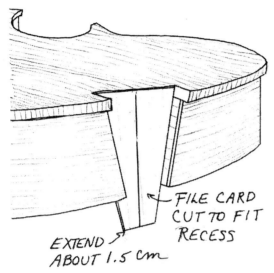

Figure 3-39

84. Cut a piece of file card to fit exactly into the neck slot at the top of the body. Allow the bottom of this card to project about 1.5 cm below the bottom edge of the rib. Mark a centerline on the card (Figure 3-39).

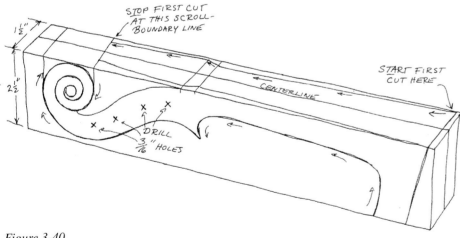

Figure 3-40

85. Use a block of maple with the dimensions shown in Figure 3-40 to form the neck/pegbox/scroll unit. If two ¾" boards have been laminated, a centerline was automatically created. If a solid block of wood is used, draw a centerline.

86. Cut out the full-sized pattern for the neck/pegbox/scroll unit.

87. Bend a piece of carbon paper, carbon side down, to fit over the top and two sides of the wooden block.

88. Fold the pattern on the dotted lines and place it over the carbon paper-covered block. Use a few pieces of tape to hold it securely.

89. Trace the pattern on both sides and the top of the block.

90. Drill four ³⁄₁₆" holes at the positions indicated with an "X". These holes will be enlarged and shaped with a peg-hole reamer in Step 161.

91. Place the block upright on the table of the band saw. Starting at the base of the neck, saw the sides up to but not beyond the scroll line. Follow the arrows in Figure 3-40. Do not cut down on the scroll boundary line to release the side pieces yet.

92. Turn the block on one side and use the band saw to cut along the profiles of the scroll, pegbox, and neck.

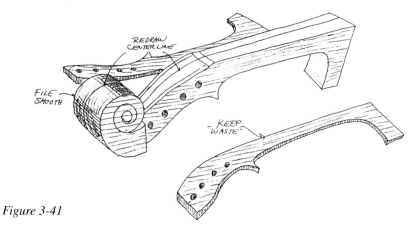

Figure 3-41

93. Turn the block upright again and use the band saw to cut in from both sides along the scroll boundary line so that the side pieces can be removed (Figure 3-41). Do not throw these pieces away because they are useful as spacers at various times when the neck has to be fastened in a vise for shaping.

94. Use files and sanding blocks to smooth all the sawn edges on the scroll, pegbox and neck.

95. Re-mark the centerline of the pegbox and scroll.

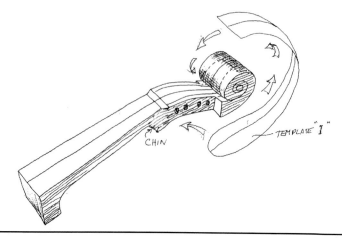

Figure 3-42

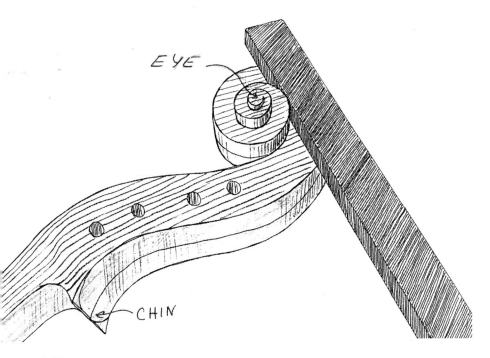

Figure 3-47

104. Starting at the side of the pegbox, use a flat file to smooth the scroll all the way up to the eye. The edge of the rising curve must be kept perpendicular to the flat surface of the scroll as it spirals upward. Again, check to see that both sides of the scroll are identically shaped.

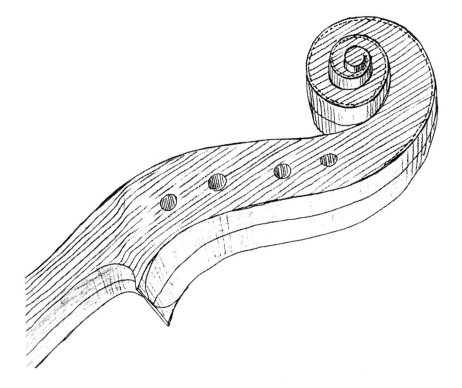

Figure 3-48

105. From the edge of the eye, mark a ¹⁄₁₆" wide border down to the edge of the pegbox (dashed line on Figure 3-48). When the scroll is undercut, the border area will remain untouched (flat).

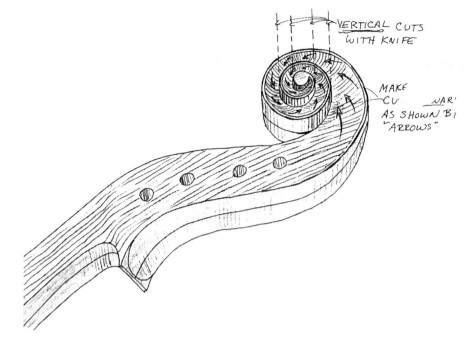

Figure 3-49

106. Use a knife to make *vertical* cuts following the curve of the scroll from the eye to the start of the peg box. Do not try to cut to full depth too fast. Instead, make repeated, short, slicing cuts as you go around the spiral (Figure 3-49).

107. Use small gouges of varying sizes to cut inward from the drawn border line toward the rise of the scroll.

108. Repeat Steps 106 and 107 until the scroll has been pleasingly shaped. Examine the scrolls of several finished violins to determine the degree of undercutting you find most attractive.

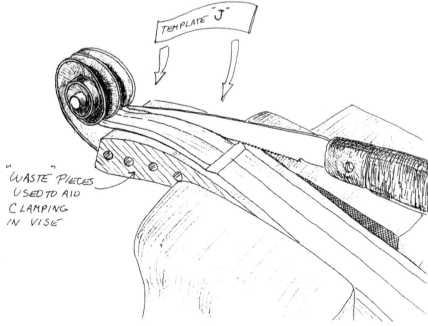

Figure 3-50

).With the aid of the waste pieces from Step 93, clamp the neck in the
⌐ shown in Figure 3-50. Use a knife-saw to cut downward as far as
⌐n the inner lines of the pegbox. These cuts can also be made
⌐ing knife.

110.Use a ³⁄₈" chisel in combination with more downcutting of the knife to
remove waste wood from the pegbox. Use *Template J* to determine the
finished depth of the pegbox cavity.

111.The sides of a pegbox sometimes split when tuning pegs are twisted
in. Prevent this from happening by gluing reinforcing pieces of veneer to
the inside walls of the pegbox. Cut two pieces of ¹⁄₃₂" veneer to the shape
of template "J." When they fit the cavity exactly, drill holes in them to match
those already in the pegbox sides and then glue them in place. Use small
pieces of toothpicks to press these reinforcement pieces tightly against the
sides until the glue dries.

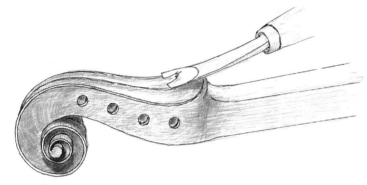

Figure 3-51

112. Use a knife, gouges, and rolled sandpaper to shape the chin and form
the grooves from the chin around the outside edge of the scroll to the
opening of the pegbox (Figures 3-50 and 3-51).

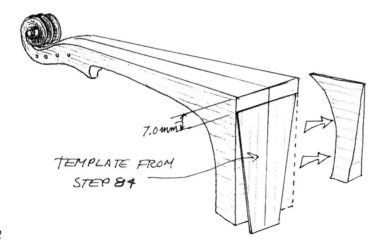

Figure 3-52

113.At the base of the neck, mark a line 7 mm from the top surface (Figure
3-52). When the neck is set into the slot in the body, the upper edge of the
top plate will be even with that height line.

114. Place the template from Step 84 on the base of the neck as shown in Figure 3-52. Trace its shape onto the wood.

115. Use a coping saw, chisel and file to cut away the waste wood on the sides of the neck base up to the height line. Trim the base of the neck to an exact fit in the body slot.

Figure 3-53

116. Cut out *Templates K and L* from the full size pattern section. Trace these patterns onto the front and back ends of the fingerboard blank (Figures 3-53 and 3-54).

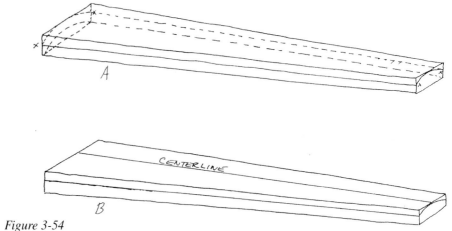

Figure 3-54

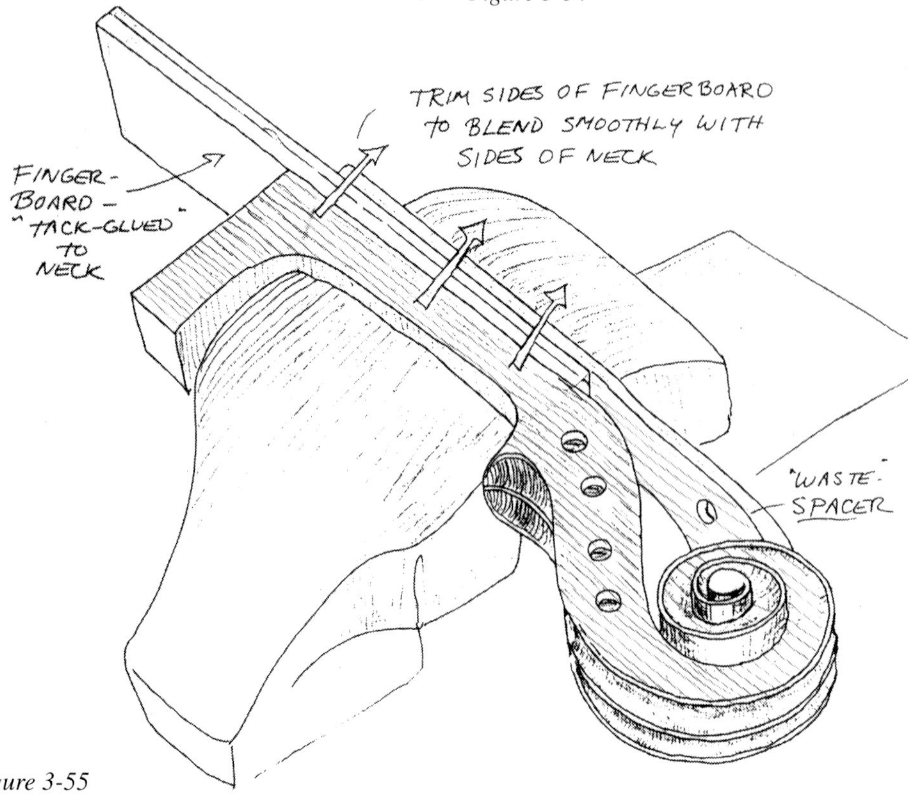

117. On the two sides of the fingerboard, draw straight lines to connect points "X" on the front and back patterns (Figure 3-54A).

118. Draw a center line on the top surface of the fingerboard (Figure 3-54B).

119. Tack-glue the fingerboard to the neck. Use just a few spots of glue so that the fingerboard can be easily removed in Step 157.

120. Use a file to trim the sides of the fingerboard to blend smoothly with the neck (Figure 3-55). It may be necessary to redraw parts of the lines drawn in Step 117.

FINGER-
BOARD –
"TACK-GLUED"
TO
NECK

TRIM SIDES OF FINGERBOARD
TO BLEND SMOOTHLY WITH
SIDES OF NECK

"WASTE-
SPACER"

Figure 3-55

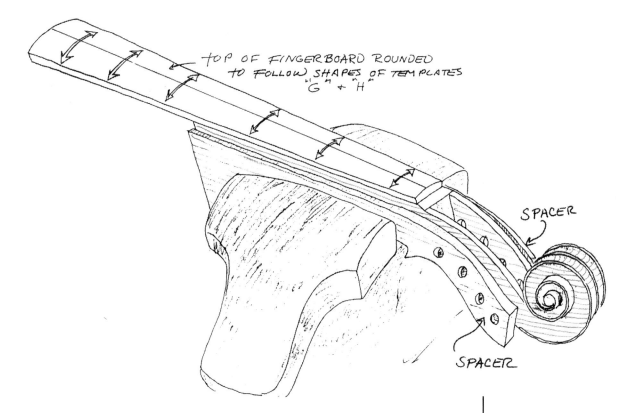

Figure 3-56

121. Clamp the neck/fingerboard assembly in the vise as shown in Figure 3-56. Waste neck cut-offs from Step 93 will permit easier clamping.

122. Use a chisel, file, and sanding block to carve the top surface of the finger board to follow the shapes of the end templates.

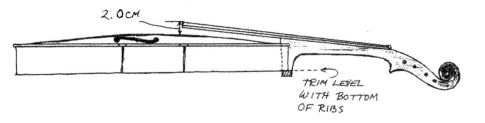

Figure 3-57

123. Fit the base of the neck/fingerboard assembly into the slot in the body. The top edge of the fingerboard should be 2.0 cm above the top of the belly. Use a file to make slight changes in the slot or the neck-base until this is achieved (Figure 3-57).

124. Hold the neck firmly in the body-slot with the centerline of the fingerboard aligned with the centerline of the belly. Check to be sure that the fingerboard top is 2.0 cm above the belly. Then, place a straight-edge across the bottom of the violin body next to the heel and mark the line at which the excess length of the heel needs to be cut off.

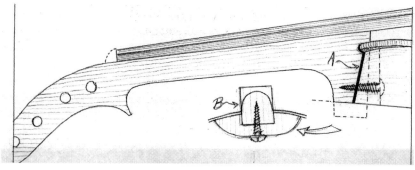

Figure 3-58

125. Cut off the excess wood at the heel. Leave just a bit extra so that later it can be filed down for an exact fit when the back plate is glued in place.

126. Use a pencil to trace a line defining the area of the neck base that will be hidden in the body slot (Figure 3-58A).

127. Draw a symmetrically-rounded shape at the base of the heel where the neck projects beyond the body slot (Figure 3-58B).

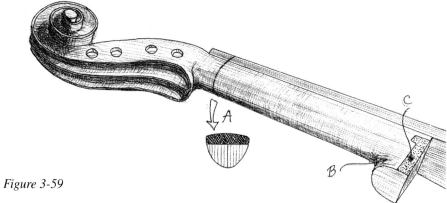

Figure 3-59

128. Remove the neck from the slot and clamp it in the vise. Carve the underside of the neck so that it follows the shape of *Template M* and blends into the fingerboard (Figure 3-59A).

129. Carve and sand the base of the neck so that it curves smoothly into the rounded shape at the heel (Figure 3-59B). Do not do any further carving or sanding in the area of the heel that is to be set into the tapered slot in the body (Figure 3-59C).

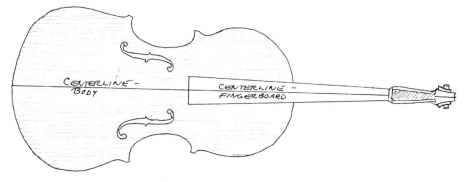

Figure 3-60

130. Apply glue to the contacting surfaces of the neck and body slot. Press the neck into place. Wipe away excess glue. Check to be sure that the centerline of the fingerboard aligns exactly with the centerline of the body (Figure 3–60) and the top of the fingerboard is 2.0 cm above the top of the belly. Use a "C" clamp to hold everything in place while the glue dries.

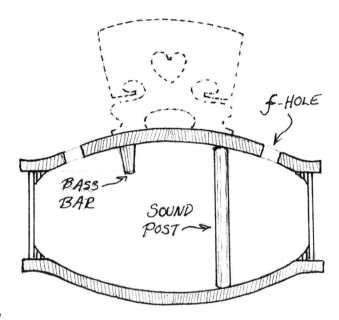

Figure 3-61

131. Insert a 1" long, round-head screw through the ⅛" hole in the front block. Screw this into the heel of the neck as shown in Figure 3-58. This screw will add a small amount of weight but it will immensely strengthen the neck-to-body join and prevent separation when the strings are tensioned.

132. File the bottom of the heel until it is exactly level with the surface of the front block (Figure 3-58).

133. The sound post can be cut to *near* final size before gluing the back plate to the ribs. Hold the back plate in place over the bottom edge of the ribs and insert a ¼" spruce dowel vertically through the front circle of the right side *f*-hole. Mark the approximate length on the dowel. Remove the dowel and cut it to that length. Remove the back plate. Using fast drying cyano-acrylate glue, *tack glue* the dowel to the inside of the belly, just below and slightly behind the location for the right foot of the bridge. Hold the back plate in place once more while looking into the body cavity through the tail pin hole. Make small changes in the length of the soundpost until it can be held in place by the slightest pressure of the back plate. *Remove* the soundpost and set it aside until final assembly (Figure 3-61).

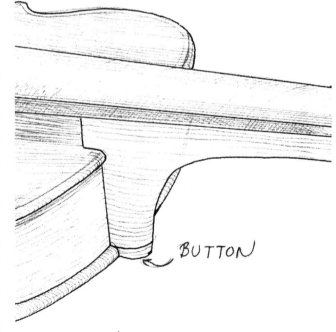

Figure 3-62

134. Apply glue to the mating surfaces of the back plate and the rib/neck structure. Place the back plate in position and clamp it in the same manner as you did for the top plate.

135. Carve and sand away the excess wood from the tab so that the button of the bottom plate blends smoothly with the base of the heel (Figure 3-62).

136. Use a knife and file to trim the bottom plate overhang so that it matches the top plate overhang of 3.5 mm beyond the ribs.

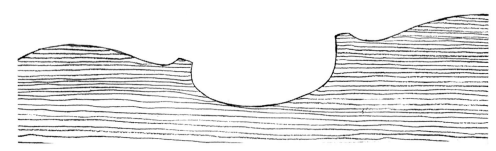

Figure 3-63

137. Mark the outlines of the four corners as shown in Figure 3-63. File them so that the corresponding top and bottom plate corners have exactly the same shapes.

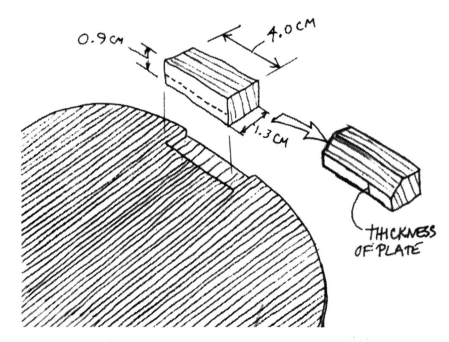

Figure 3-64

138. Set the end rest block into the opening in the belly and mark the block to show the thickness of the belly plate (Figure 3-64).

139. Use a chisel to shape the end rest as shown.

140. Glue the end rest into place.

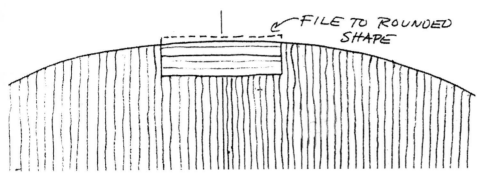

Figure 3-65

141. Use a file to make the back of the end rest conform to the curve of the top plate (Figure 3-65).

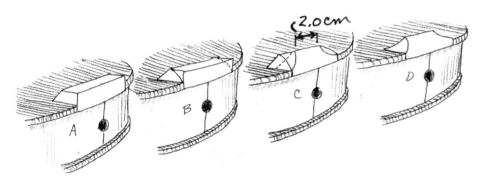

Figure 3-66

142. The end rest is now carved with a gouge and knife as shown in Steps A, B, C, and D (Figure 3-66).

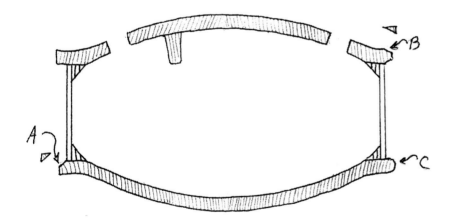

Figure 3-67

143. Use a small chisel to bevel the inside and outside edges of the top and bottom plates as shown in Steps A and B of Figure 3-67.

144. Use a sanding block to round off the plate edges as shown in Step C.

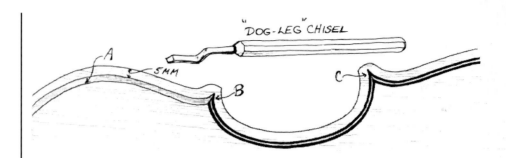

Figure 3-68

145. On the top plate, measure in 5 mm from the edge and make pencil marks around the edge at intervals of about 2 centimeters (Figure 3-63).

146. Use a pencil and draw a smoothly curving line connecting the points all the way around the edge.

147. Draw a second line inside the first. Determine the spacing of these two lines by the thickness of the purfling to be inserted.

148. Use a knife to cut straight downward on the two lines. Make the purfling groove about 1.5 mm deep. Do not try to reach that depth with one cut! Make many small, slicing cuts, especially when cutting across the grain of the spruce top.

149. Use a small, dog-leg chisel of the same width as the purfling to remove the waste wood between the two incised lines (Figures 3-68A and 3-69A). Make very shallow shavings so that the chisel does not plunge entirely through the plate. Small motorized cutting wheels are very helpful in cutting the purfling channel, but the dog-leg chisel and thin knife blade are still needed for the corners. Continue cutting downward until the channel is 1.5 mm deep.

150. Cut the channel in the back plate in the same manner.

151. The purfling strips can be purchased ready-to-use or you can make them from veneer strips. If you make your own, start by cutting the veneer into 1³/₈-in.-wide strips.

152. Use the rib form blocks to shape the purfling strips. Cut two strips of dark mahogany veneer and one strip of light maple veneer to the lengths indicated on the bout forms. Glue these together in a "sandwich" with the light-colored maple in the center.

153. Before the glue dries, clamp the purfling "sandwich" inside the form. When the glue sets, use a bandsaw to cut the sandwich into 3.0 mm wide strips. You will need four strips of each type for the back, middle and front bouts (on both upper and lower plates).

154. Set the center bout purfling strips into the grooves first. Trim away the

Purfling can be self-made as in Steps 151–153 or purchased pre-made.

excess wood on an angle at the ends where they fit into the corners of the groove, as shown in Figure 3-68B. The purfling strips must fit to the bottom of the groove. When the fit is correct, glue the strips in place. Wipe away excess glue and then use luthier's clamps to hold the strips in place as the glue dries. At this stage, the tops of the purfling strips will project slightly above the top of the plate (Figure 3-69B).

155. The front and back bout purfling strips are shaped, glued, and clamped in the same manner. The miter joints with the center bout purfling strips should resemble Figure 3-68C.

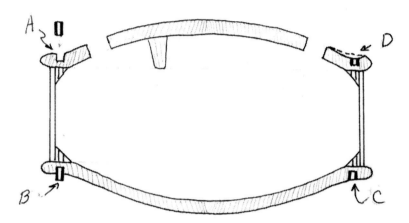

Figure 3-69

156. When the glue holding the purfling strips has set, use a small gouge and carve away the purfling that projects above the plate surface (Figure 3-69B). Also, deepen the purfling area of the plate very slightly as you cut away any glue residue (Figure 3-69D). Remove any traces of gouge marks with a scraper.

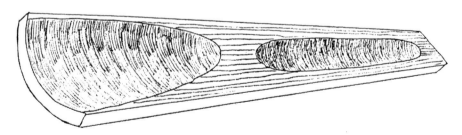

Figure 3-70

157. The fingerboard had previously been tack-glued to the neck for preliminary shaping. Now, remove it for further work. Insert a thin knife blade between the neck and fingerboard to wedge them apart.

158. Brace the inverted fingerboard against a block nailed to the workbench and use a gouge to carve away the underside as shown in Figure 3-70. This will reduce unnecessary weight.

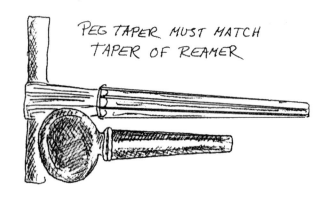

Figure 3-71

159. If maple has been used to make the fingerboard, give it several coats of ebony black stain. Sand lightly between each coat to obtain a very smooth surface.

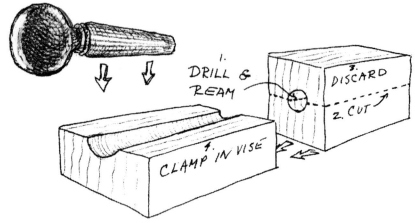

Figure 3-72

160. Shape the four tuning pegs to match the taper of the reamer that will be used to enlarge the holes in the pegbox. Use a block of wood with a groove cut into it to hold the pegs as they are filed to shape (Figures 3-71 and 3-72).

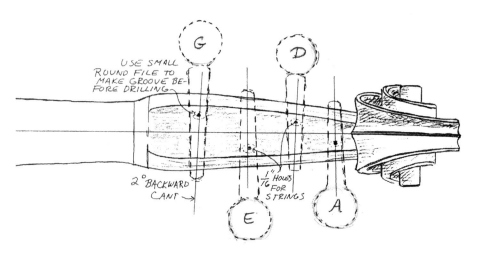

Figure 3-73

161. Ream the pegbox holes to shape *after* the tapers of the pegs match the taper of the reamer. When the pegs are correctly fitted, their shafts will have a slight backward cant (2°) toward the bridge (Figure 3-73). This will help to prevent the peg from slipping under string tension. Ream the holes slowly and carefully, adding slight, sideways pressure to introduce the 2° backward cant shown. Check the fit of the pegs frequently. Stop reaming when the finger grips are about 2 cm from the outer sides of the pegbox. The peg tips will project about 3 mm from the other sides of the pegbox. Each peg must be individually fitted to a particular pegbox hole. Mark them to prevent mix-ups.

162. Drill a ¹/₁₆" hole through each peg for the string. To make drilling easier, use a small, round file to make a shallow groove on the peg shaft a short distance from where it touches the inside wall of the pegbox.

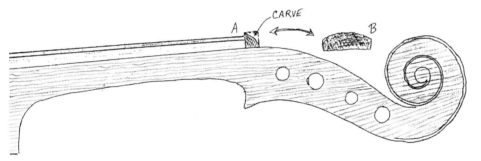

Figure 3-74

163. Use the reamer to shape the tail pin hole in the back block.

164. Protect the surface of the violin with colored varnish. This can be purchased ready-to-use from luthier suppliers or made in the following manner: (a) Select a light-colored stain. Pour a small amount into a clean container and allow it to stand, exposed to air, until most of the solvent has evaporated. (b) Add some clear varnish and stir the mixture. (c) Apply two or three thin coats of this colored varnish to the entire violin. Allow each coat to dry thoroughly. Sand lightly before the next coat is applied.

165. Glue the fingerboard to the neck. Use thinned-down hide glue because the fingerboard may be replaced eventually. Use spring clamps to hold the fingerboard in place as the glue dries.

166. Glue in place at the end of the fingerboard (Figure 3-74) the piece of ebony or maple that will form the nut.

167. File the top of the nut to match the curve of the fingerboard. The top of the nut should be about 1 mm higher than the top of the fingerboard.

168. Carve and file the front of the nut to match the shape shown in Figure 3-74A.

169. Mark the locations of the string grooves in the nut as shown on *Template N.* Use a small, triangular file to cut very shallow grooves so that the strings will not sink below the top edge of the nut.

Figure 3-75

170. If the fingerboard and nut are maple, apply a coat of polyurethane to them. Do *not* use polyurethane on the body of the violin.

171. Fit the bridge across the top plate between the notches of the *f*-holes. The bridge will have to be shaped to fit your violin. Carve and sand the feet to exactly match the curve of the belly (Figure 3-75).

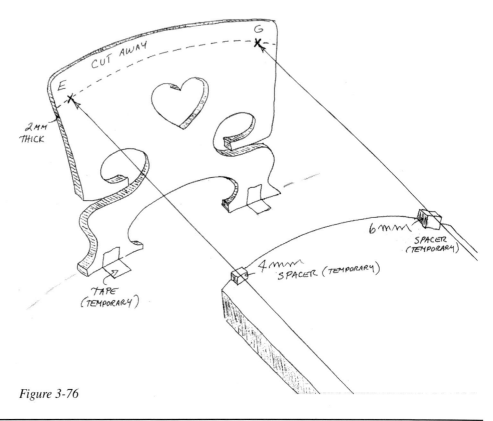

Figure 3-76

172. Use strips of tape to temporarily hold the bridge upright in the correct position between the *f*-hole nicks (Figure 3-76).

173. At the top of the fingerboard on the E string side, place a 4 mm thick spacer. Place a 6 mm thick spacer on the G string side.

174. Run a straight edge from the top of the nut over the top of the 4 mm spacer. Where the straight edge touches the E string side of the bridge, make a mark. Do the same thing on the G string side of the bridge.

175. Remove the bridge. Place the top curve of *Template O* on the bridge from point E to point G and trace the curve on the wood (dashed line on Figure 3-76).

176. Cut away the waste wood above the curved line on the bridge.

177. Sand the bridge until the top edge is 2 mm thick.

178. Use Template O to locate the points where the strings will touch. Again, make *small* nicks so that the strings will ride on the bridge and not sink deeply into it.

A pincer-type (sound post) setter can be purchased from violin supply companies.

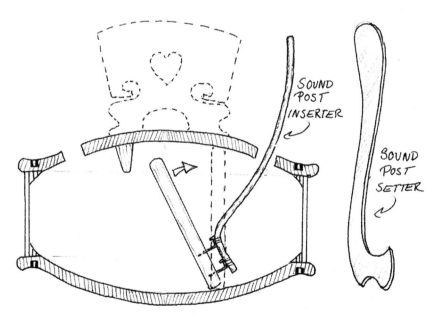

Figure 3-77

179. The soundpost, which was cut and shaped to an approximate fit in Step 134, is now set in place. First, impale the soundpost on the double pointed soundpost inserter, then insert the sound post into the violin through the right hand *f*-hole. A thread tied to the sound post and exiting through the *f*-hole allows for easy removal of the post if it falls over during this process. Peer into the body cavity through the tail pin hole as you position the post as shown in Figure 3-77. Insert the sound post setter through the same *f*-hole. Hook the top of the sound post and pull outward until it wedges snugly in place between the top and bottom plates. The soundpost

should stand vertically under the E string foot of the bridge and about 1 cm toward the back when viewed through the right side *f*-hole. The post should not be wedged so tight that it distorts the plates. Nor should it fall over easily. Do not glue the post in place as it may be necessary to make slight changes in its position to achieve the best sound. The post is moved only when the string tension is released.

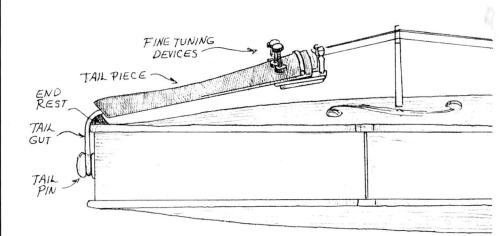

180. Insert the tail pin in the bottom block. Adjust the tail piece tail gut, which fits over it, to the proper length by turning the small nuts on its threaded tips. The relationship of the tail piece to the end rest shown in Figure 3-78.

Figure 3-79

181. Rub a soft pencil point in the string grooves of the nut and bridge for lubrication. Install the strings as directed by the manufacturer. Be aware that as you tighten the strings, the bridge will start to tip forward! Watch for this during the tuning process and, using both hands, carefully keep adjusting it so it stays perpendicular to the surface of the belly. If you neglect to check this, the bridge may snap down with great force and crack the top plate!

182. Celebrate your creation by playing the Bach *Chaconne* or *Old Joe Clark*.

Pattern Section

The following section contains the full size patterns, templates and reference drawings needed to construct the violin as shown in the preceding text.

Due to the size of the originals, some drawings have been spliced to run across a two page spread.

Simply make a photocopy of each page. Then fold or cut each page to line up the registration marks. We suggest you then glue these patterns to a stiff paper backing for durability.

TOP PLATE (BELLY)

UNDERSIDE VIEW - SHOWING THICKNESS CONTOUR LINES (MM)

TOP PLATE (BELLY)

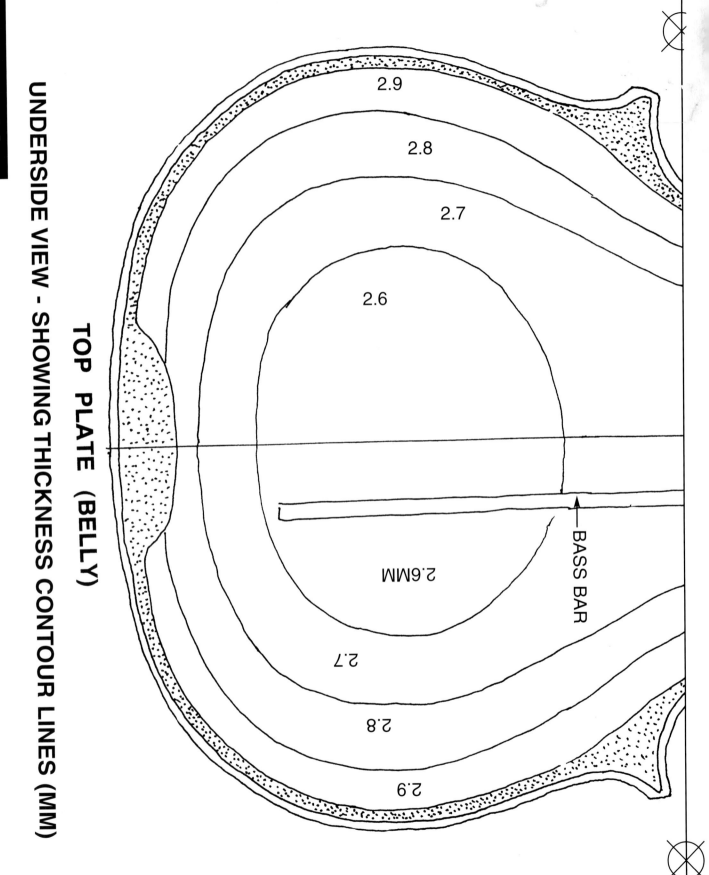

2.9

2.8

2.7

2.6

2.6MM

BASS BAR

2.7

2.8

2.9

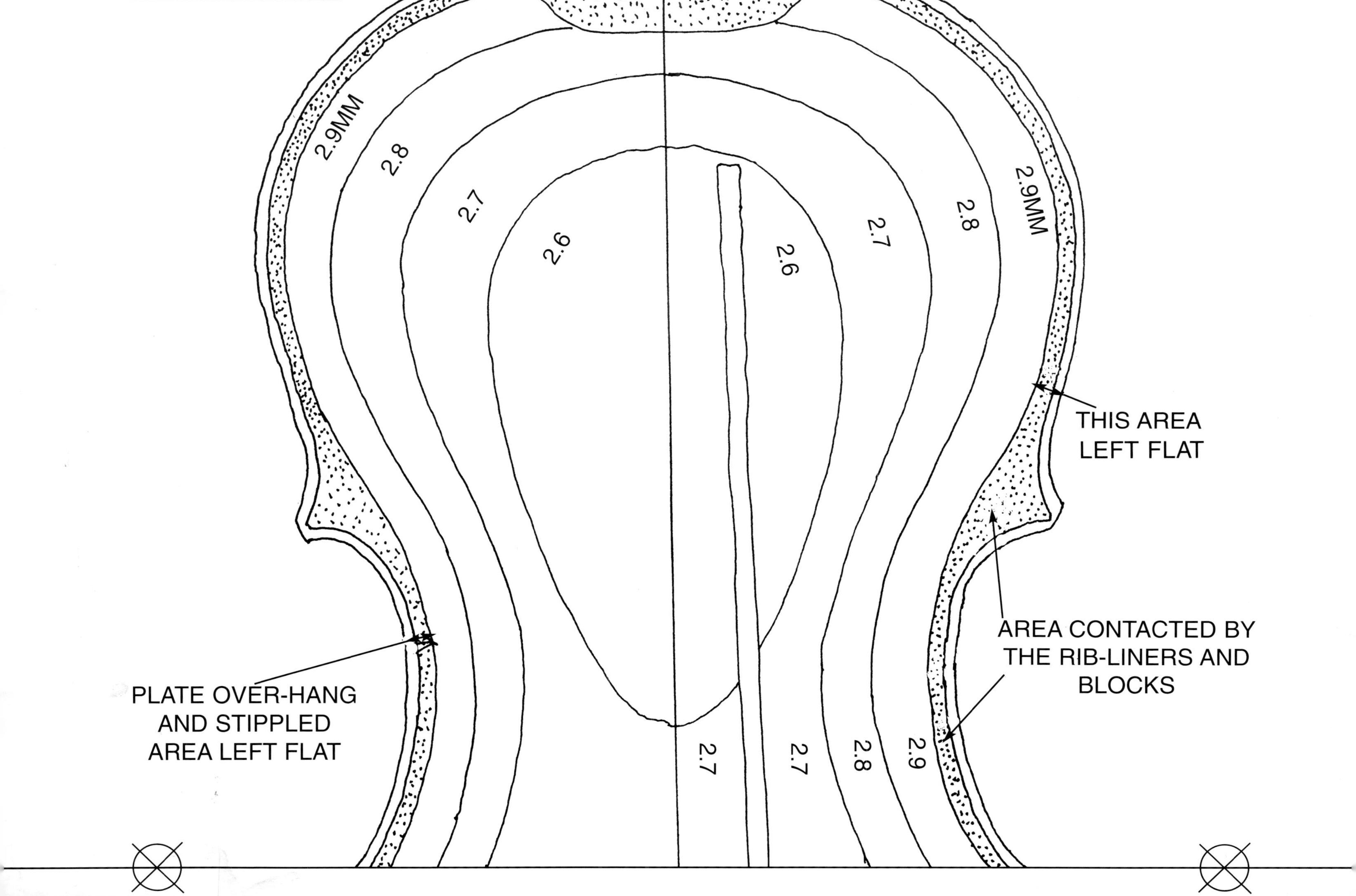

PATTERN

PLATE OVER-HANG
AND STIPPLED
AREA LEFT FLAT

2.9MM

2.8

2.7

2.6

2.7

2.6

2.7

2.8

2.9

2.7

2.8

2.9MM

AREA CONTACTED BY
THE RIB-LINERS AND
BLOCKS

THIS AREA
LEFT FLAT

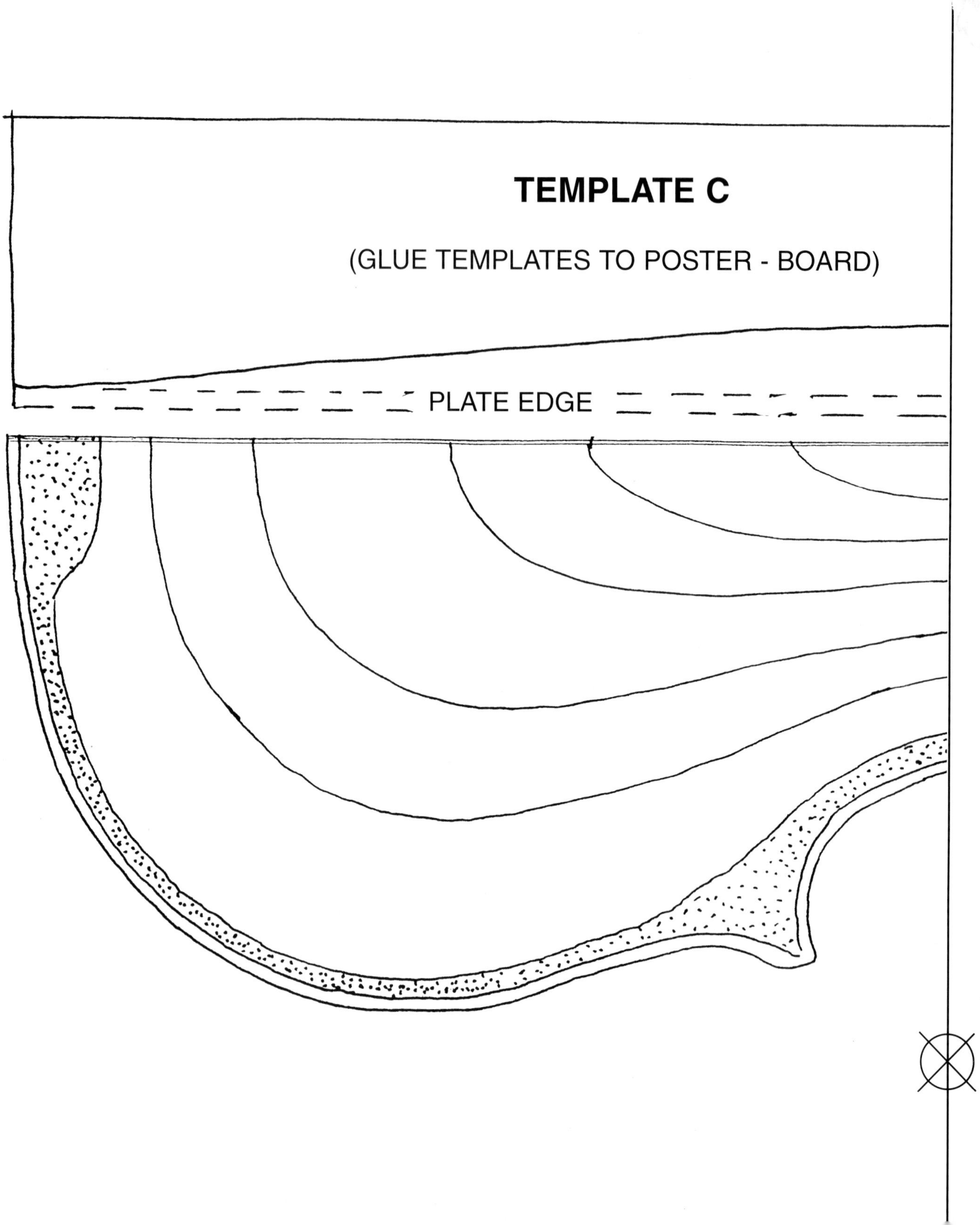

TEMPLATE C

(GLUE TEMPLATES TO POSTER - BOARD)

- - - - - - - PLATE EDGE - - - - - -

BOTTOM PLATE (BACK)

58

PLEASE SEE PAGE 67 FOR TEMPLATE D, E AND F.

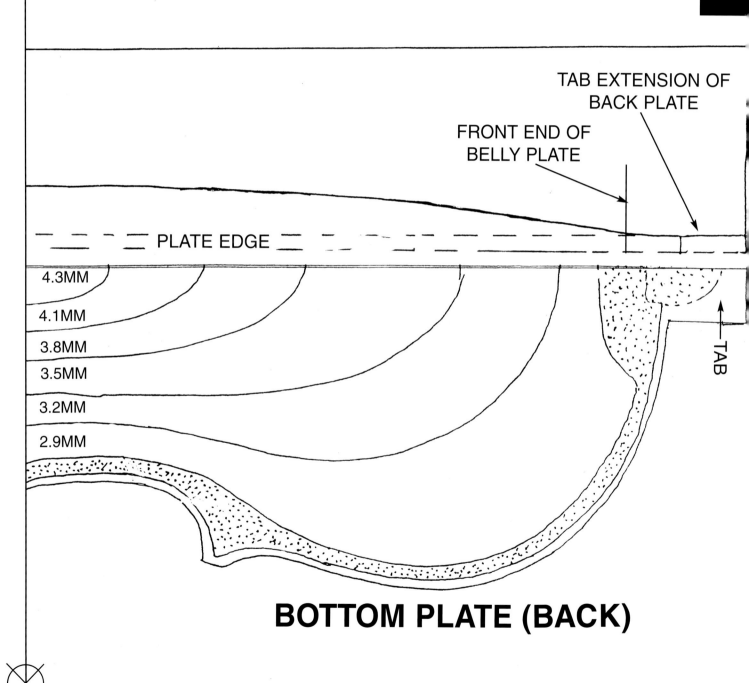

TAB EXTENSION OF
BACK PLATE

FRONT END OF
BELLY PLATE

PLATE EDGE

4.3MM

4.1MM

3.8MM

3.5MM

3.2MM

2.9MM

TAB

BOTTOM PLATE (BACK)

BUILDING FORM PATTERN

60

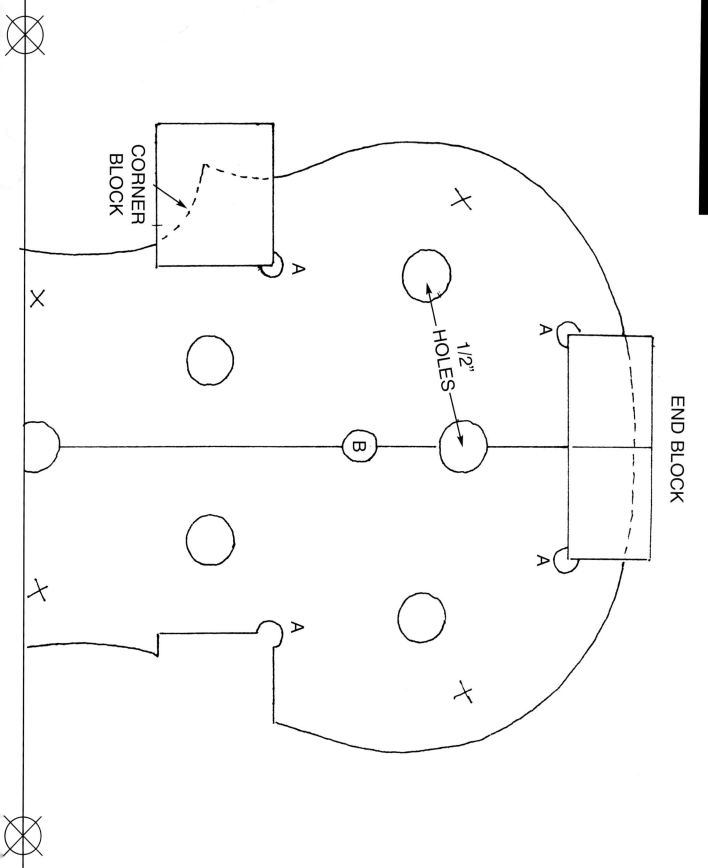

CORNER BLOCK

A

1/2" HOLES

B

A

A

END BLOCK

A

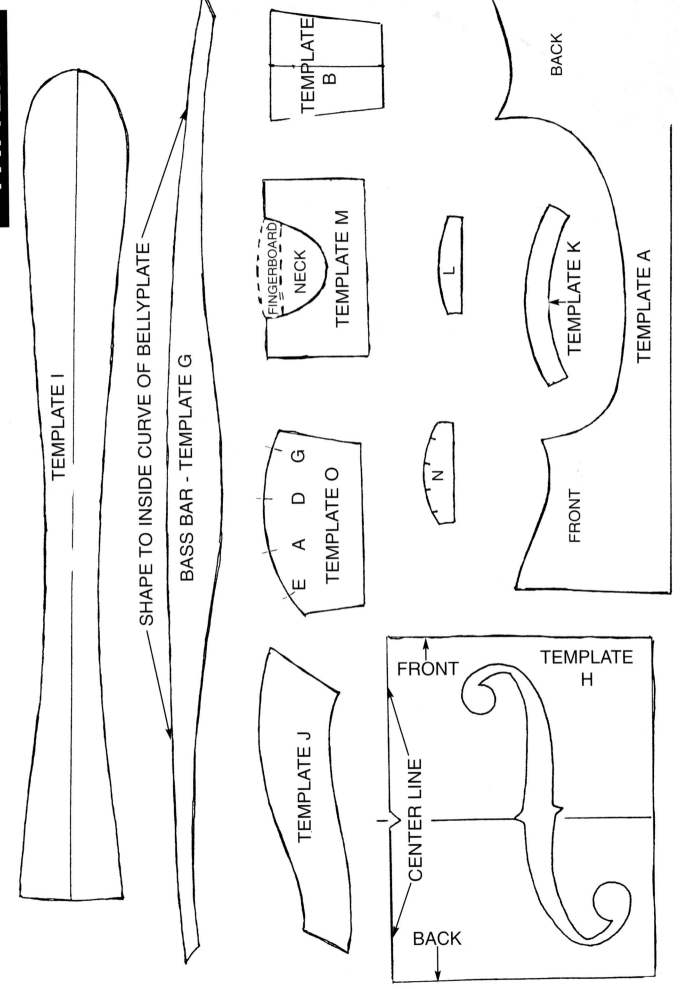

TEMPLATE I

SHAPE TO INSIDE CURVE OF BELLYPLATE

BASS BAR - TEMPLATE G

TEMPLATE B

FINGERBOARD

NECK

TEMPLATE M

TEMPLATE L

TEMPLATE K

TEMPLATE A

BACK

FRONT

E A D G

TEMPLATE O

N

TEMPLATE J

FRONT

CENTER LINE

BACK

TEMPLATE H

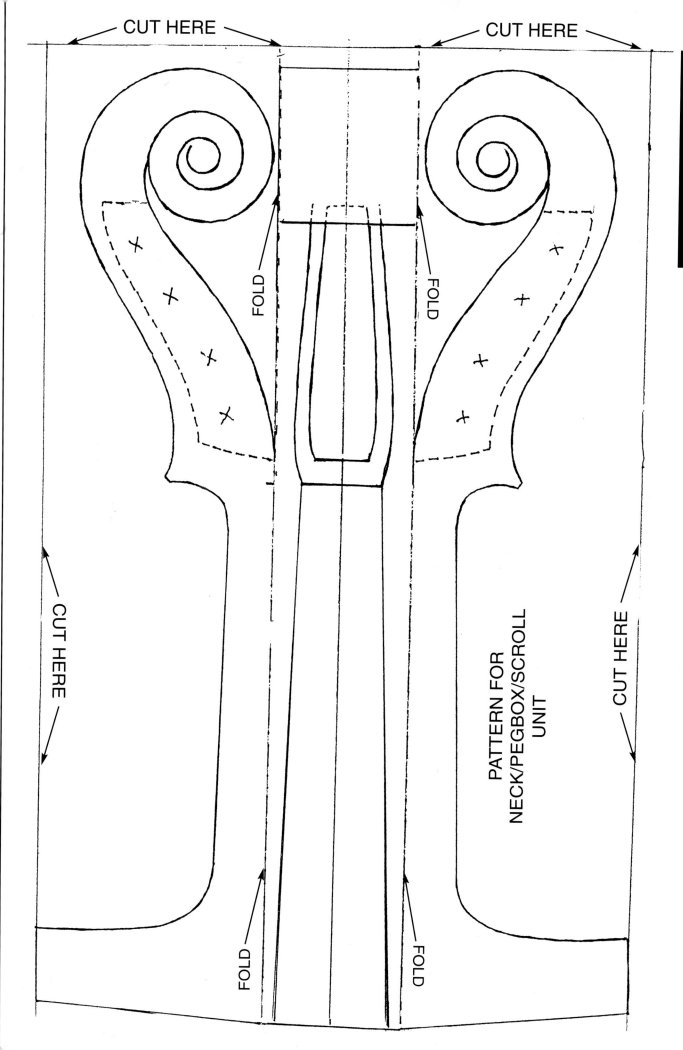

CUT HERE

CUT HERE

PATTERN

FOLD

FOLD

FOLD

FOLD

CUT HERE

CUT HERE

PATTERN FOR
NECK/PEGBOX/SCROLL
UNIT

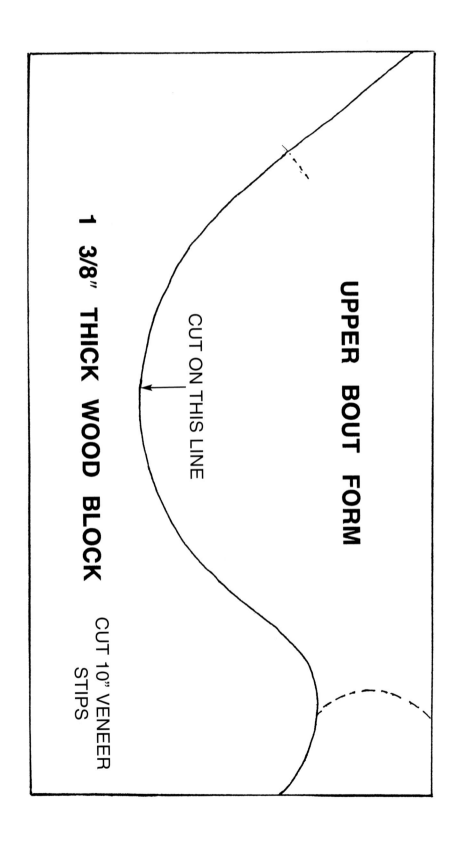

UPPER BOUT FORM

CUT ON THIS LINE

1 3/8" THICK WOOD BLOCK

CUT 10" VENEER STIPS

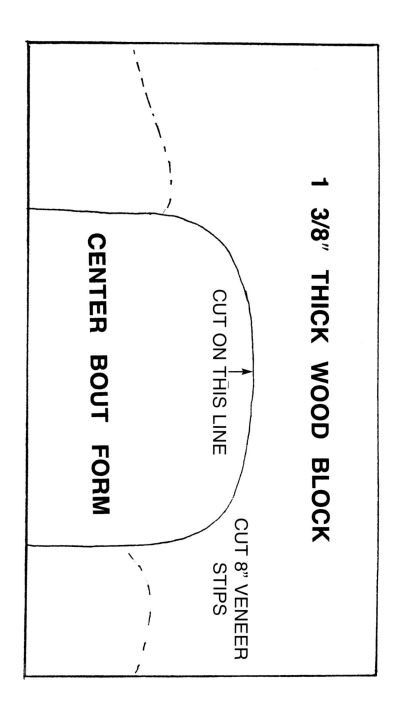

1 3/8" THICK WOOD BLOCK

CUT ON THIS LINE

CUT 8" VENEER STIPS

CENTER BOUT FORM

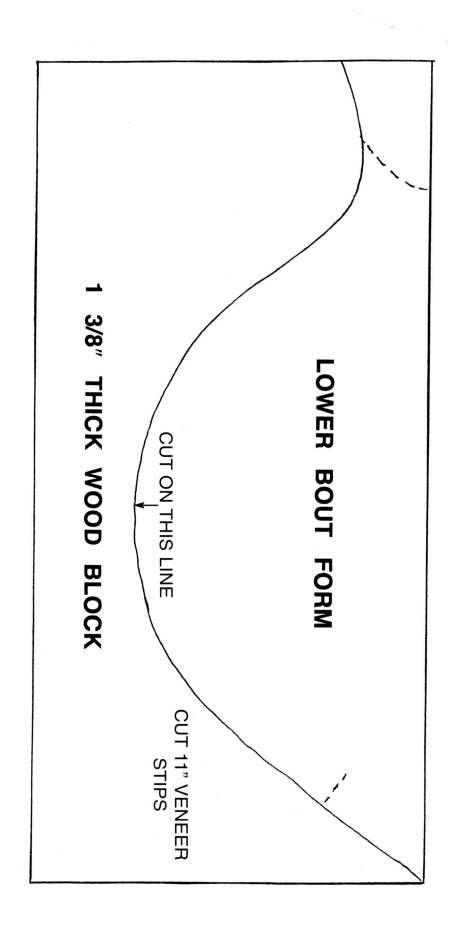

LOWER BOUT FORM

1 3/8" THICK WOOD BLOCK

CUT ON THIS LINE

CUT 11" VENEER STIPS

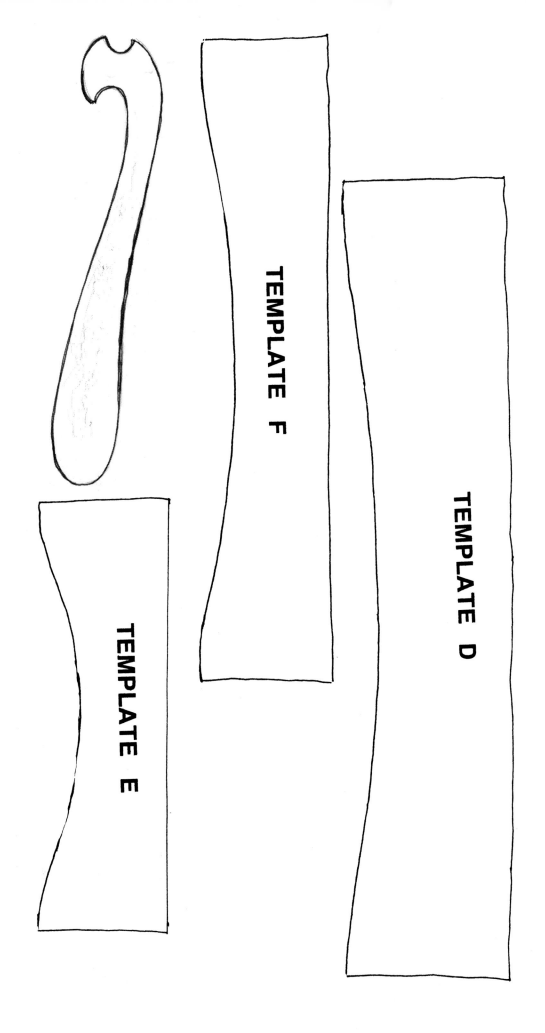

TEMPLATE F

TEMPLATE D

TEMPLATE E

67

The following companies are sources for imported and domestic wood, tonewoods, veneers, tools, varnishes, materials, accessories, and books.

Battenkill Tonewood
Box 780
Arlington, VT 05250
802-375-9965
curlywd@compuserve.com

Hammond Ashley Bass Violins
19825 Des Moines Memorial Dr.
Seattle, WA 98148
800-787-4642
www.bassviolins.com

International Luthiers Supply Inc.
PO Box 580397
Tulsa, OK 74158
918-835-4181

International Violin Co., Ltd.
1421 Clarkview Rd.
Baltimore, MD 21209
800-542-3538
www.internationalviolin.com

Metropolitan Music Co.
4861 Mountain Rd.
Stowe, VT 05672
802-253-4814
www.metmusic.com

Old Standard Wood
4925 CR 351
Fulton, MO 65251
573-443-2904

Stewart MacDonald's Guitar Shop Supply
21 N. Shafer St.
Athens, OH 45701
740-592-3021
www.stewmac.com

The Wood Well
2023 East Sims Way
Port Townsend, WA 98368-6900
www.thewoodwell.com

PERIODICALS

Strings
www.stringsmagazine.com

The Strad
www.thestrad.com

ORGANIZATIONS

Violin Society of America
www.vsa.org

Catgut Acoustical Society
www.marymt.edu/~cas